The Graduate's Guide to Life and Money

2nd Edition

By Bill Pratt, MBA

From the Author of
Extra Credit: The 7 Things Every College Student
Needs to Know About Credit, Debt & Ca$h

Published by
Viaticus Publishing
4104 Sterling Trace Dr
Winterville NC 28590 U.S.A.
www.TheGraduatesGuide.com

ISBN: 978-0-9818702-9-8

Printed in U.S.A.

Viaticus Publishing.
   The Graduate's Guide to Life and Money, 2E / by Bill Pratt.
   ISBN: 978-0-9818702-9-8

This publication is designed to provide accurate and authoritative information with regard to the subject matter covered. It is sold with the understanding that the publisher is not engaged in rendering legal, accounting, or other professional advice. Since individual situations may be fact dependent, and if expert advice is required, the services of a compctcnt professional should be sought.

This book is available at quantity discounts for bulk purchases.
For information visit www.inceptia.org/books.

Contents

Foreword

Congratulations! You are, or soon will be, a college graduate. As the president of one of the largest organizations that helps college students achieve the dream of a higher education, I've seen first-hand how completing college can improve lives. I've also seen the devastation that happens when students don't learn the money management skills they need to avoid financial mistakes. *The Graduate's Guide to Life and Money* will help you start on the path to financial success as you begin your journey to career success after you leave college.

Bill Pratt shares my passion for teaching college students to succeed financially, not just while they're in college, but for the rest of their lives. As a former credit card company executive, Bill saw how financial mistakes can ruin lives. He left the for-profit world to teach full-time at East Carolina University, where he's helping create a robust personal finance program for college students to address their unique needs. He authored *The Graduate's Guide* to give college students a handy, easy-to-read reference for managing money and staying out of financial trouble both in, and after, college.

If you are a college student (or the parent of one) who wants practical advice on preparing for life after college and avoiding those tricky financial dilemmas you'll face (like deciding to rent or buy, finding student loan payment options that won't bust your budget, or divvying up expenses with your roommate, for instance), then *The Graduate's Guide* provides a mega-dose of information you'll actually be able to use.

Completing college is your first step to a better life. *The Graduate's Guide* can help you have a better financial life.

Randy Heesacker
President
Inceptia

Acknowledgments

To Inceptia, who provided resources and expertise for the college financial aid and student loan concepts and examples I've included in the book.

To Dr. Anna Filippo for helping me in the process of editing.

To my business partners. We really can make the future better through financial education.

To my family, Christy, Casey, Riley & Phoebe. Thank you for everything. I have been blessed with an incredible family.

To every one of my supporters, too numerous to mention. Thank you so much for everything. You have each contributed more than you know.

To the students and graduates who will read this book. Good luck as you transition from 'learning' to 'doing.' I am confident you will succeed personally and financially.

Before You Begin

Congratulations! You've graduated, and now you are finally on your own. The next question is, "What do I do now?" You've just had four years (give or take) of all night study sessions, (you know, the ones where you do everything *but* study), finals, parties and a diet consisting mostly of pizza. And let's not forget about the free rent or the college loans. That's right; mom and dad no longer have to keep paying your room and board. Plus, if you borrowed money you get the added benefit of paying back your loans... with interest. Don't worry, I'm not here to take away all of your fun. What I want to do is show you how to enjoy your new life without going broke.

It's amazing that after taking so many required courses you weren't ever really taught how to handle your finances. "What? I just spent $40,000 (possibly of mom & dad's money) over the past four years to prepare for my future and I didn't learn a thing about my own finances?"

Sadly, even if you were an economics, accounting, or finance major, most of the fundamentals of *personal* finance were still left untaught. Apparently, it's more important to know that Andrew Jackson was the seventh president than to know how to balance a checkbook. Well no offense to President Jackson, but the only way he is going to be able to help me with my finances is if I have a bunch of twenty dollar bills with his picture on them in my pocket.

You have already taken a financial step in the right direction by reading this book. If the book was a gift, then at least you opened it. Sadly, we don't even realize how little we know until we have to start making smart financial decisions. For instance, an insurance agent might want you to buy a whole life variable annuity with a conversion clause. "It's the greatest thing for your family. You do want to protect them don't you?" Hello! What if you don't even have a family yet?

Perhaps the car salesman has a great deal for you, "You can lease it and only pay for what you use. Your payments will be much lower." Yeah, and best of all, you'll have to do it again every three years for the rest of your life!

What I want to do in this book is show you all the things you need to know to make the best financial decisions without making any of the mistakes I did. Everything from finding a job and an apartment, to making the most of your 401(k) to paying off your student loans will be covered in this book. All you have to do is follow along, and maybe do a few action steps (try not to think of them as homework, but rather as… well… *learning exercises*).

I've tried to lay out this book in a very logical order. It's designed so you can go through the book cover-to-cover. However, if you feel certain chapters are not important at this time (maybe you already have a job, or you don't need a car any time soon), just skip them. You can always come back to them later. Some of my comments in this book were written under the assumption that you have (or are about to be) graduated from college. However, if you are a high school graduate and are going directly into the workforce, or you are just somebody under the age of thirty-five, then all of the principles are just as relevant.

First of all, if you had to move back in with mom and dad, don't feel bad. It's happened to the best of us. I, too, had to move back in with my parents for about six months. With rental prices still out of reach in some areas and high unemployment almost everywhere, moving back home for a while is becoming more common. When I moved back home it was because I was having trouble finding a job.

Just remember, your goal is to move out of your parents' house as quickly as possible, without ruining yourself financially. I think I speak for most of us when I say "as *quickly* as possible." It's really difficult after four years of social freedom to suddenly move back in with the folks. A word of advice, if you do move back in with them remember it is *their* house and they are doing *you* a favor. Respect that and things will go much smoother.

I want to emphasize the phrase "without ruining yourself financially," because there are a few fundamental points that must be made.

- Your parents have more money than you
- Your parents are smarter than you (just in case my parents read this)
- Your parents have been working for more than 20 years
- Your parents have been accumulating stuff for more than 20 years

- Rent is not cheap
- Paying your own bills stinks
- Your whole paycheck is no longer "play" money

I will discuss each of these points in more detail later in the book. For now, let's talk about what to do if you are living at home. You have to understand that as much as your parents love you, it is inconvenient when you move home. No, I don't mean for you (although that may be true). I mean for them. Having an extra person in the home is an added stress, and it forces your parents to make changes to accommodate their extra resident. A great reason you should plan to move out in less than one year.

Also, don't spend every dollar of your paycheck like you did when you were in college. If you have found a job then you are probably making more money now. Take advantage of this opportunity to save your money. Trust me, once you are out on your own, there will be few opportunities to save like this again. Besides, the quicker you save money, the sooner you will be able to afford your own place.

The first part of this book is going to help you cover the basics. We are going to look at searching for a job, writing a resume, and impressing people at the interview. Some people have great personalities and do well in interviews, but their writing skills are somewhat lacking. Others can write an incredible resume, but have bad interviewing skills. Both of these skills must be combined to get the job you want. You also have to know what you want from your job. We'll talk about that when we discuss the job search.

The second section of the book is designed to help you with money basics - all those things taken for granted, such as where you do your banking; how to write a check; and what all those numbers on your pay stub mean.

You'll also learn how to set up a reasonable spending plan and use your money wisely. Don't worry; I am not talking about a strict budget where every dollar has to be tracked. I'm talking about knowing your money habits so you can have more freedom to spend without the worry.

The third section of the book will help you find an apartment or buy a house. But there's more to your apartment than just paying rent. I'll go over a few "tricks" to help you save time and money by doing some things yourself. I'll also offer some especially helpful hints for when you own your own home. If you need one, you'll also learn the ins and outs of buying or leasing a car.

In section four, we talk about how money actually works. That's right, we'll knock out those college loans and credit card balances in no time. As we discuss retirement and investments, you'll learn how to make your money work hard for you. You will also learn about insurance and what you do and don't need. Not to be left out, we'll delve into the ever-dreaded topic of taxes.

The final section emphasizes *personal* finances. We'll go over a few things life will throw at you such as marriage and children. You'll also gain a better understanding of the differences between men and women when it comes to money. I'm no relationship expert (just ask my wife), but if you go in knowing a few key differences about how you and your significant other communicate and how the two of you view money, you'll be way ahead of the game.

I want to make this as easy as possible while still giving you the information you need to succeed in the real world. We all have great potential, and we can either squander that potential, or we can live life to its fullest. I want to give you the tools to excel in the world of personal finances without having to first dig your way out of a big hole. Basically, I plan to cover all the things they don't teach you in school about real life and money.

Part I: Your Career

*"Your degree makes you marketable;
what you do with your degree makes you successful."*

1. **Nobody Majors in 'Unemployment', it Just Comes With Your Diploma**

   ➢ Learn where to find the best job listings

   ➢ Learn where to apply

   ➢ Discover what you are really interested in doing

2. **Get Noticed, Get Hired, and Get Paid!**

   ➢ Write a cover letter that will get you noticed

   ➢ View a sample cover letter

   ➢ Write the resume that will get you an interview

3. **Ace the Interview**

   ➢ Learn how to follow up after an interview

   ➢ Impress the interviewer to guarantee that job

   ➢ Practice several sample questions that are typically asked

   ➢ Learn what *not* to do or say in the interview

1

Nobody Majors In 'Unemployment', It Just Comes With Your Diploma

S ince you are reading this section, I am going to assume you are either unemployed or underemployed. You're not alone; it takes many college students months to find a job after they graduate. Think about it; you are competing against more than two million other people who just graduated with you across the country. The point of this chapter is to help you find that first (or second, or third) real job. What do I mean by "real job?" Basically, any job you actually *want* to do, or one requiring your degree.

To begin, you should have some idea of what you want to do. There are all types of resources available including personality tests and self-evaluations to help find the best job suited for your wants and skills. Once you get a general idea, you should evaluate your education, skills, and experience. From here you can either choose an industry or an occupation. For instance you may want to be in the banking industry, or you may want to be a financial analyst for a large company in any industry.

Don't think you have to stick to a particular career just because it relates to your major. Many employers have started looking for people with certain types of skills with the understanding they can always train them for the specifics of the job. For instance, a math teacher could be hired to be a statistician. The skill sets needed to do both overlap. A retail store manager could be hired to help run a department in a telemarketing company since many of the customer service and management skills overlap. The specifics of the job – related directly to telemarketing – can be easily learned. The demonstrated ability to manage, sell, or handle customers is easily transferable.

I don't want to gloss over this topic too quickly. You really should be thinking about a career more than just a job. When you first graduate you might be willing to take just about any job that pays.

You may actually be forced to take just about anything if your job search takes too long. You might not find your dream job right away, but you could find yourself on your dream job track. In other words, you may start at the bottom, but you could be in the right industry with room for advancement.

If you are interested in obtaining a federal job, you should visit the Office of Personnel Management's (OPM) job site at *www.usajobs.gov.* At this site, you can search for federal jobs by location, pay level, department, current job openings, and more. Recent college grads can select "Entry Level Professional" and search by location. There are a number of jobs located outside of the Washington, D.C. area, so do not exclude this site just because you do not want to move near the nation's capitol.

Even if you are looking for a private sector job, you may want to apply for a few government jobs. With federal government jobs it may take several months before you get interviewed. That is why you must start early.

Searching for a private sector job is a bit more complicated since you may be searching dozens of different companies. There are a number of useful Web sites. Following is a list of some of the more prominent national ones:

Hotjobs – *www.hotjobs.com*
Monster – *www.monster.com*
Careerbuilder – *www.careerbuilder.com*
College Grad – *www.collegegrad.com*
True Careers – *www.truecareers.com*
College Recruiter – *www.collegerecruiter.com*

There are also sites that list jobs in specific industries and are dedicated to particular genres, such as non-profits, education, etc. Appendix A has a list of web addresses for specific professions.

You can also search for jobs using your local newspaper or the local paper in whatever city that interests you both in print and online. You can search by job category, experience needed, or even salary, just like using one of the national job searches. Unfortunately salary is not listed very often. If it says "entry level," just assume you'll be ranked somewhere between the cleaning crew and the interns.

If you already know which companies interest you, visit their Web site. Most companies post their current job openings online. You may be able to find an open position before it is posted in newspapers or on job search sites. The sooner a company receives your resume, the greater your chance of getting an interview.

Don't just send your resume to that one job that sounds perfect. You should send it to many different employers at once. In fact, if you are unemployed, there is no such thing as too many interviews (unless they are scattered around the country). While larger companies collect resumes electronically, it is still a good idea to get a paper copy in the hands of the decision makers. You should definitely use quality paper (unless you are faxing your resume).

Don't forget to post your resume online at one or more of the previously listed Web sites. But use caution when doing this. Your employer could see your listing or - even worse - you could become the victim of identity theft. Make sure the site is credible and has security measures before posting any personal information, including your full name.

Okay, so what if you've tried the usual sources and still had no luck? There are still a few things you need to do. Consider this your first action step:

1). Network – Tell people you are looking for a job. This includes friends from college, your professors, your parents' friends, people in your church, and just about anyone else you know or meet. Don't start rambling about your job search to random people on the subway, however, unless you are pursuing a career as a professional pest.

Think about it this way. If you worked somewhere and knew there were openings, or you knew someone who was hiring, would you help one of your friends if they asked? Of course you would. Most people will. What most people cannot do is read your mind. You have to ask first. You will be surprised how much that can help.

2). Call a placement agency – There are several employment firms that do more than just hire temporary workers. On the other hand, a temporary position would not be such a bad idea. After all, you can gain valuable experience at several different firms. Sometimes what begins as a temporary position can end up as a full-time career. Even getting a part-time job wouldn't hurt, especially if the experience is relevant to your career goals. The added bonus is you still have plenty of free time to attend interviews.

3). Contact companies that interest you – Most available positions are not posted to the public. In fact, it seems the better the job, the less likely it is to get posted or advertised as an opening. Think about it, it makes sense. If you are an employer offering a very attractive position, you could probably fill it without even posting the job. Why? Because a qualified candidate has either asked their friend about positions and they referred them, or because several qualified people already contacted the employer to seek out potential openings. In the next chapter, we discuss how to send your resume to companies that have not listed any open positions.

While many companies now require a formal application process, having already made connections still gives you a huge advantage. At the very least, the hiring manager can look for your resume and application. Even better, they may choose to write the job announcement based on your resume, so you will already come out not only qualified, but among their top candidates.

You need to research some companies. If you know the career field that interests you, research companies in that field. You may have already visited a few companies' web pages looking for job openings. You have to be prepared before you write your cover letter (Chapter 2). Find out as much as you can about each company.

Create a list of interesting facts about the companies. For instance, you should know their primary industry, where they rank in that industry, annual revenue, number of employees, and so on. Most Web sites have a link that says "About the Company" or something similar. You can also visit *www.hoovers.com*, which will provide a great source of information. You may find out how and why the company began (what need they were trying to fill), the original owners, the company mission, and their vision statement. Getting these facts will come in handy later as you send a resume and go on an interview.

The best way to begin is to set up a notebook or spreadsheet and list each company you would like to apply to. List the contact person (if there is one), phone number, where you heard about the job opening, location of the company, etc. After that, note when you mailed your resume and any other correspondence. Leave space to list the dates letters were sent, such as follow up letters after the interview, as well as room for any telephone call details.

Once you have your notebook or spreadsheet ready, you can move on to the next step. Make any necessary adjustments to your resume to reflect what the company is looking for in an employee and be sure to gear your cover letter to the specific job.

What happens if you follow the advice in this book and get a job but instead of being excited you realize you are in the wrong job? After all, you accepted the job offer because it seemed perfect. You were told, "You only have to work 40 hours and can come in to work late if you want. It's a pleasant atmosphere and a family-friendly work environment." Then you actually get there. Suddenly, you find yourself working late every evening, maybe even weekends. Your boss is constantly watching over your shoulder and teamwork ends up meaning you get to do all the work for the whole team. You can't stand the thought of staying there for another minute, but you can't afford to quit. Now what?

Look for another job. It really is that simple. No law says you have to stay with your employer just because they hired you (unless you signed a contract – in which case you will have to negotiate your release with at least a neutral letter of recommendation). Believe me, if the situation was reversed and the company was having problems, they would not hesitate to cut your position. In fact, if you are the newest hire, you may be the first to go.

Most businesses operate on what is known as "employment-at-will." This means your employer can come to you at any point and say, "I'm sorry, but you are just not working out here," and fire you. On the flip side, you have the right to say to your employer at any time, "I'm sorry, but *you* are not working out," and quit. Okay, don't do it quite like that. You do not want to burn any bridges. You never know when you may need that manager as a reference or as part of your career network later, especially if you stay in the same industry. In fact, you may end up wanting to work for that company again later (which is why you should always give at least two weeks' notice). Also, make sure you have another job offer before you quit. Otherwise, as you struggle to pay rent, your landlord may come to you and say, "I am sorry, but you are not working out here – now get out!"

Do not be too disappointed if your first job does not work out. You just need to update your resume to show your current position and any additional skills you have gained. Be sure to update your resume at any online site where your information is still posted. Start researching new companies or even contact ones to which you had previously applied. In a few short months things may have changed. Don't take it personally if you were not their first choice for the job, if the company *now* wants you. If you are offered the job you want, take it. Prove to them they were mistaken for not choosing you initially, and make them so glad they finally did.

You may be wondering how it will look if you only held your job for a few months. Don't worry about it. A good employer will look past the fact that your first ever post-graduate job did not work out. The key is to be able to explain your reasons for leaving the job.

Interview questions are discussed more in Chapter 3 (sample questions and answers are listed in Appendix D), but the most important thing is to not badmouth your present employer. Emphasize the positive points of your present employer, but focus on what makes the company that is now interviewing you unique.

If you find yourself in a bad job, you really should try to stay in it for six months to gain some marketable experience. If six months is not doable try to gut it out for at least three months so it *looks* like you gave it a shot. Of course, I realize some jobs are just so horrible even three months seems like an eternity. I once had a job so bad I began searching for a new one after just six weeks. I was able to find another job less than a month later.

If you start to jump from job to job every couple of months you may need to reconsider your career choice. Perhaps you were a business major and you now find that sitting behind a desk all day just isn't what you are cut out to do. Maybe you were an elementary education major but you realize now that working with children causes more headaches than you first imagined. Sometimes it's impossible to predict how well you will be able to fit with your career choice.

To find a better fit for your personality, you have several choices. As mentioned before there are personality tests available to help you find the type of job that might fit your personality. You can also go to sites such as *www.livecareer.com* or *www.careerpath.com* and take an online personality test that should help you select a career path based on your interests. In some instances you may find that a career counselor is worth the cost.

Another option is just to search the Internet. You will be surprised to find the amount of information available about what to expect in certain professions. Sometimes you can find discussion boards geared towards specific professions. Browsing these forums or even posting your own questions could give you a better idea of what to expect as you begin your new career. Don't be surprised if your interests change over time. As humans, we are constantly changing: Just call it part of growing up.

Chapter 1 Action Steps

Your first action step is as follows:
  1) Network,
  2) Call a placement agency, and
  3) Contact companies that interest you. If you want to earn a little extra credit (and this will only benefit you), begin a journal of companies you want to work for or visit three career sites and write down some information about 10 jobs or more that interest you.

Chapter 1 Summary

❑   Finding a job takes time and requires some work.

❑   Focus on a career, not just a job.

❑   Create a fact sheet about each potential employer.

❑   Use friends, family, former roommates, etc. to network.

❑   You can always look for a new job, even after you begin your first one.

2
Get Noticed, Get Hired, Get Paid!

I know, you're probably such a charmer you can't imagine why anyone out there wouldn't want *you* to work for them, right? Well, no one is going to know how great you are without first meeting you. The way you set up that first meeting is with your resume and cover letter. You have to get a foot in the door by using your writing skills, then you can charm away at the interview.

Most people spend so much effort on their resume, they forget about their cover letter. In some cases, your cover letter may actually be more important than the resume. The cover letter (sometimes called a letter of interest) is a quick overview of why you want the job, where you heard about it, and why you should get it. Make no mistake; the cover letter is your one chance to make a good first impression with a prospective employer. In fact, it is the cover letter that could help you get the interview.

To begin, use quality personal stationery if you have any. Quality does not include anything with kittens, teddy bears, or sports team logos. I'm talking about professional looking stationery. Something you might see as business letterhead. If you don't have any, use the same quality paper you used for your resume. Do not use two different types of paper for your cover letter and resume. It will just make you look disorganized.

Limit your cover letter to one page. For most jobs, good communication skills are essential. If you can't say what you want in less than one page, the employer may see that as a sign of someone who can't get to the point. You also need to leave space between paragraphs. The cover letter should look professional and should be easy on the eyes. If too much information is crammed onto a page it will look cluttered. Trust me, if your cover letter gives the reader a headache, you will not get an interview.

If possible, you want to address the cover letter to a <u>person</u>. A simple "Dear Sir or Madame" or "Dear Personnel Department" might not cut it. Try to contact the company if you can and ask for the name of the person most likely to be reviewing job applicants. If you know someone who works for the company, ask them to whom you should address your cover letter. If you absolutely cannot find the name of the person who will be reviewing your resume, use one of the following:

- Dear Hiring Manager
- Dear Hiring Committee
- Dear Human Resources
- Dear [Name of company]

Your first paragraph should be something that will interest the reader. You could mention something about the company:

> Recently I have been researching the top performing companies in the Washington, D.C. area and I have noticed your company is constantly ranked among the top ten in sales...

If you spoke to someone prior to sending your resume:

> In response to our telephone conversation on Tuesday, January 20th, I am forwarding my resume to you.

If you were referred to the company by someone who knows the hiring manager:

> Bob Smith, your senior staff accountant, recommended that I contact you regarding any openings in your finance department.

If you are responding to an advertisement or a job posting:

> I am writing in response to your advertisement in the News-Post on January 20th for an entry-level economist.

If you are applying for a position more than one month before graduation, you may want to mention your availability:

> In eight weeks, I will be finishing my bachelor's degree in economics at Frostburg State University…

The next couple of paragraphs should state why you are writing to them, and why they would be crazy not to ask you for an interview (don't use those exact words). You could begin by using something like one of the following:

> I am writing because I believe my educational background would allow me to excel at your company.

> As a recent graduate in computer science, I feel my up-to-date training and skills could add to your company's industry ranked, first-rate technology department.

You could also point out specific skills that may not be mentioned on your resume, but were specifically listed in the posted job announcement:

> In addition to my work experience, as detailed on my resume, I have four years' experience talking one on one with people as a volunteer counselor for…

> My work experience as an Order Specialist has really allowed me to pay special attention to details in order to satisfactorily meet my customers' expectations.

Ending paragraph:

The entry-level economist position is an outstanding opportunity with a highly respected company and I would welcome the chance for an interview to discuss your needs and outline my strengths in person. I can be reached during regular business hours at (301) 555-5555, or by email at kwerk@TheGraduatesGuide.com. Thank you for your time, and I look forward to meeting with you.

Sincerely,

Kent Werk

Be sure to leave four spaces between the word "Sincerely" and your name. You need to sign your name in this space.

To see how to put it all together, refer to Figure 2-1 to view a sample cover letter.

Having a good resume is the first real step to finding a job. In fact, throughout your entire career you should always keep your resume updated. You never know when an opportunity might come knocking or when your boss will call you into the office to tell you, "You've been doing a great job here, but corporate office says we have to let some people go." You know -- the corporate equivalent to, "It's not you, it's me…"or "We're just not working out, but we can still be friends."

To write a good resume you must first know what to put into one. Your name is always a good start. You also need to provide at least two ways to contact you - preferably three. For example, your phone number, email address, and postal address would allow the prospective employer to contact you whichever way they prefer. Remember; don't make anything too fancy, unless you are applying for a graphic design job. Otherwise, stick with something that looks professional.

Next, you should detail your education, your degree, and your GPA (unless it screams, "Study? You mean like *after* class?"). Also, include any salutations, such as Cum Laude, or Summa Cum Laude, etc. You should include both your major and your minor. You could even list your separate GPAs; just make sure you also include your overall GPA if you are going to do this.

Next, identify your relevant work experience. If you don't have any (sorry, but washing cars or babysitting does not automatically qualify you to be a financial analyst), then list your past three jobs. Be creative when referencing your responsibilities at those jobs and try to make them relevant to the job for which you are applying.

My street address
City, State Zip

Date

Mrs. Martha Washington
Title
Organization
Street address
City

Dear Mrs. Washington:

I am writing in response to your advertisement in the News-Post on March 20th for an entry-level economist. In eight weeks, I will be finishing my bachelor's degree in economics at Frostburg State University.

I am writing because I feel my educational background would allow me to excel at your company. After reviewing my resume, you will find that I have a strong background in economics. During my 3-month summer internship with X-Stat I was able to put real-life application to the theories I was learning in college, while also adjusting to the dynamics of a full-time job. In addition, I have also been an active member of the Economics Honor Society. As a student, I have earned a reputation as a solid performer who always pays close attention to details.

The entry-level economist position is an outstanding opportunity with a highly respected company and I would welcome the chance for an interview to discuss your needs and outline my strengths in person. I can be reached during regular business hours at (301) 555-5555, or by email at kwerk@TheGraduatesGuide.com. Thank you for your time, and I look forward to meeting with you.

Sincerely,

Kent Work

Kent Werk

Figure 2-1: Sample Cover Letter

Being creative does not mean lying. It just means looking at your responsibilities through the eyes of someone who is making the hiring decision. For instance, if you worked at a car wash, one of your tasks may have been to "track weekly sales." Or, perhaps you "organized the equipment and ordered new supplies as needed." That indicates responsibility and organization skills. Both of which are important to almost any job.

Always use action verbs to describe what you did. In the previous paragraph I used the words "track" and "organized." A bad example would be "kept track of weekly sales," or "supply cabinet organizer." Also, if you are currently still employed, you should use present tense (*"Track* weekly sales"). If you no longer have that job or those responsibilities, you should use past tense (*"Organized* the equipment").

The best way for a recent college graduate to label their work experience is by simply using the word "Experience" as the header for one of the sections of your resume. This will allow you to include internships and volunteer work. Be sure to label them as such. You want to describe the responsibilities and accomplishments most relevant to the job for which you are applying.

Another section of your resume could include any specific courses or seminars you think the employer would find especially useful. For instance, if you had a business course that focused on computers, you may want to mention it. Also, if you attended a conference or seminar pertinent to the position you want, you should list those as well. If the name of the course or seminar is not self-descriptive, list a few of the important topics that were covered.

Do not forget to list your accomplishments or achievements. This includes any awards or special honors you may have received. It may be useful to describe the award. Winning the John Doe Achievement award may be great, but unless you tell your employer it was for your dedication to improving the efficiency of the student government, they could assume it was an award for holding onto a burning match the longest at a fraternity party.

While it may seem like a lot has to go on your resume, you must be succinct enough to fit it onto one page at this point in your career. As your career grows and you gain more experience with increasing responsibilities, you may have to expand your resume to two pages. Technology majors are an exception to this rule since they want to list all the programming languages and certifications they have accumulated. It is not uncommon for the resume of a new technology graduate to spill over onto a second page.

At the end of the resume you should include the phrase "References available upon request." Of course, you better have your references available upon request. If the company is seriously considering you as their next hire, they may very well want to check your references. They may ask for your references prior to an interview, but they will most likely wait until afterward.

You should already have three to five references available. You want at least one professional reference, such as a former employer, the director of wherever you volunteer, or whoever was in charge of you during your internship. You should also have a personal reference, which could be a coworker, teacher or clergy member. The dean of your school would also make an excellent choice. You want to make sure you let the person know you have listed them as a reference so they don't hesitate when your potential employer calls and asks them about you. You also want to be confident they will give you a good recommendation.

Sometimes if you do a good job on a project or you are a volunteer, your supervisor will say, "If you ever need a reference, feel free to use us." Unless they said that with a sarcastic tone as they locked the door behind you, take them up on it. If it has been a few months, remind them of their offer, "Hello, this is Kent Werk... Yes, that's right I interned for you this past summer. When I left, you said I could use you as a reference. With your permission I would like to take you up on your offer. I'm applying for [whatever the job title]. If you would be willing to give me a positive reference, I'll send you a copy of my resume so you can get an idea of what else I've been up to. Thank you again."

Are you ready for your second action step? (At least it's not a pop quiz.)

Chapter 2 Action Step

1. Review your resume. Follow the rules you just read. Look for action verbs, check any misspellings, check for consistency (either you use periods at the end of each bullet point or you don't). Update it to include your current job. Pretend that your dream job just became available and you will need to submit your resume tomorrow.
2. Write a cover letter. Make up a job opportunity if you have to. The important thing is to get experience writing a cover letter. Once you get the format and the wording correct, it will be easy to update when a real job does come along.
3. Purchase some quality resume paper. This will become less important as you grow in your career, but right now your prospective employer has little to go on. You are asking them to take a risk and hire you.

Chapter 2 Summary

❑ You will need a good cover letter and resume.

❑ Use the same quality and type of paper for both.

❑ Your cover letter and resume should each be no more than one page with plenty of white space.

❑ (If you are an information technology graduate with several certifications, then the one-page approach may not apply.)

❑ Always check your resume for consistency, grammar, and spelling.

❑ Check your resume again.

❑ If you are going to use someone as a reference, ask him or her first.

3
Ace the Interview

Thanks to your excellent resume and cover letter you are now getting calls by the dozens from companies that really want to interview you. Maybe that's a bit of an exaggeration, but you should be getting at least a few phone calls by now.

When you answer your phone, be polite and professional. In the event someone calls to set up an interview, you don't want to answer your phone, "This is Bob, wussup?" If you have listed a landline phone shared by family members or roommates, let them know you may be receiving professional phone calls. It may be best to list your cell phone first on your application materials. The same professionalism applies to your voicemail. One of my college friends had a crazy voicemail message that greeted callers with, "Welcome to Bob's house of torture." This is great for laughs from your friends, (well, at least from *his* friends) but not so great when a prospective employer calls. This is also important after you have your interview and are waiting for that inevitable job offer. Again, use your cell phone as your primary contact number. Just use a professional (not sarcastic) voicemail greeting.

Use the notebook or spreadsheet created in Chapter 1 with information about the companies you researched. It should be located somewhere you can get to it quickly along with your calendar. That way you can easily recall to whom you are speaking, and determine when would be a good time to setup an interview. Get directions and confirm the date and time. If possible, ask who will be doing the interview, and get the proper spelling of his or her name(s).

In some instances, an employer may conduct a telephone interview. Usually a telephone interview is nothing more than a pre-screening. The employer wants to know if they are interested in you enough to have a face-to-face interview. Normally, you will receive a call to schedule a phone interview. In the rare event you receive a phone call and the person says they would like to conduct a telephone interview now, use a stalling technique to catch your breath and find the company in your notebook. Just say, "Yes, that would be fine. If you don't mind, I need to step into a private room," or "Now would be a great time. I just need to set the groceries down so I can talk."

The point is you want to be as relaxed as possible, which is difficult when you are caught off guard. In the event you are having a telephone interview, remember these key points:

➢ Do not chew gum, smoke, or chew your fingernails.

➢ Remove yourself from distractions such as the television, radio, Chihuahua, etc.

➢ If you tend to talk fast when you get excited, make a conscious effort to slow down. It is a little more difficult to understand someone over the telephone.

➢ Sit down. It will make you less nervous.

➢ Write down the contact information from the interviewer, including their name, title, telephone number, and email address (if possible). Make sure you get the proper spelling of his or her name.

➢ Get the name and number of the interviewer's secretary/assistant if possible. Call him or her after the interview to confirm all spellings, etc. are correct.

➢ Ignore call waiting.

If you are not having a telephone interview, or you had one and were asked to come in for a one-on-one, you need to be prepared. Have extra copies of your resume and your cover letter. You only need two copies of your cover letter. The first will be for your reference, and the second will be available to the interviewer in the event your original cover letter was lost.

You should have at least two copies of your resume for every interviewer, or a minimum of five (another reason to ask who will be interviewing you when you receive that first phone call, as you may be told there will be three or four interviewers). If you are told a committee of three will interview you, make six copies of your resume. This will allow you to distribute one copy to each member, in case they do not already have a copy, and have extra copies if needed.

You should arrive at the interview with a nice folder (such as one of those leather ones or vinyl ones if it is not cracked). Inside the folder have a notepad, two pens, and several copies of your resume. You should also have a list of questions prepared that you will ask the interviewer as well as any relevant company data you may find useful during the interview. If you are traveling farther away from home or from your hotel, you may want to bring a briefcase. Bring a soft briefcase, black, brown, or burgundy. Women should not carry a purse if they bring a briefcase. Choose one or the other. You are just there for an interview; you don't want to look like you're moving in.

You are probably anxious to know what to wear to the interview. First make sure you are presentable. Be clean and showered, but don't go in smelling like you're marinated in a bottle of cologne or perfume. You should smell nice, but your aroma should not be detectable from two blocks away. Some people are allergic to perfumes, and your interviewer may be one of them. Make sure your fingernails are clean and trimmed. Women should have their hair neatly styled and men should be cleanly shaven or have their facial hair neatly trimmed. (Women, if you need to neatly trim your facial hair, just close this book now. My advice will be of no use to you.)

Obviously, you don't want to wear shorts and a t-shirt. To play it safe, think conservative. If you look into the mirror and think, "Wow, I *am* hot!" change your clothes. You aren't going on a date, you're interviewing for a job. Khakis and a button up won't do the job, even if that's what everyone at the office wears. You need to look professional, not office casual.

Men need to wear a suit. Dark colors such as black, navy blue, and charcoal gray work best. You should use a white or light color shirt. Do not use pastels, and do not wear shirts with stripes. Make sure your tie matches but is not too flashy. Do not wear a tie with cartoons, wildlife, or words. Your socks should match your suit (black with black, blue with blue, etc.). Your shoes should be either black or brown, and should match your belt.

For women, a business suit is perfectly acceptable as well as a professional looking dress, or a skirt that is about knee length or longer. Whether a man or woman does the interview you will make them feel uncomfortable if you show too much skin. Women should also wear dark colors such as black, gray, or navy blue. A dark brown suit is also perfectly acceptable. Avoid any jewelry that dangles, and avoid wearing too much makeup. A good rule of thumb is less is better (except for the skirt).

Be on time. That is the best advice I can give you about an interview. I will never forget when I was in Student Government and we were interviewing for a position: one of the applicants was 10 minutes late.

During the whole selection process, one of the interviewers on the five-person panel kept saying, "but he was late." In the end, he did not get selected.

Even better than just being on time, you should be early. Don't be "I have no life and camped outside your office all night," early, just be between 10 and 20 minutes early. If you are unfamiliar with the building or the city, you need to add extra time in case you make a wrong turn. Believe me, in some of the large downtown buildings, you can easily get lost. You should arrive at the office where the interview is to take place about 10 minutes early and no later.

Before the interview (perhaps the day before), make a dry run. Simply drive or get a ride to the location of the interview. You may also want to go inside the building (if it's open) so you can see if there is a directory listing the name of the person whom you'll be meeting for the interview. Of course, be careful with the dry run. A friend of mine did her dry run on a Sunday and went to her interview on Monday when the traffic pattern was much different due to rush hour. The street she used on Sunday was used as a one-way street during rush hour (going the wrong way, of course). This is a common problem in large cities.

You must also allow for the possibility of a detour because of construction or an accident. If some unforeseen circumstance causes you to be late (despite the fact you left in plenty of time), call the interviewer and let them know of your situation. You should apologize profusely, but not sound whiney. Just explain that there is an accident (or whatever the case may be) and you are sincerely sorry, but you do not believe you'll make it to the interview on time. Ask if there is any possible way they could still hold the interview when you arrive. You could even ask if there are alternative directions to their location so you can get around the obstruction.

Once you arrive for the interview introduce yourself to the receptionist (if there is one). Tell him or her you are there because you are scheduled for an interview and with whom. Be sure to sound confident but not arrogant. Also, if you shake anyone's hand, especially the interviewer, use a nice firm handshake. Don't crush any bones but your hand should not feel like a dead fish either. Try to be as calm and professional as possible.

If you are asked to wait, be prepared to wait for a long time, in case the "boss" is in a meeting. You can look through your notes or browse an industry-related magazine. One should fit inside of your notebook. If you have a briefcase, you could have a book inside. Be sure the book is appropriate. A popular novel would be a good choice; a racy romance novel or the technical manual from a sci-fi convention would not.

Here comes the hard part. Your name has just been called. What do you do? You could run. *Don't forget your briefcase.* Or, you could stand up, smile, and follow the person back to the interview room. On your way back to the room, take a few deep breaths, and remember you are there to sell yourself, and to make yourself a valuable commodity.

Smile and firmly shake the interviewer's hand. If the interviewer is of the opposite sex, wait for them to extend their hand first. If you do extend your hand first, don't worry about it. The worst move would be to pull your hand back and make yourself look weak. If they begin to fumble around for a copy of your resume, or if they appear to not have a copy handy, offer them one.

There are two types of questions at the interview. There are the questions the interviewer asks you and the questions you will ask the interviewer. We will discuss both types of questions, as well as those that should *not* be asked.

At the end of the interview, you will usually have the opportunity to ask a few questions. If you do not want the job, do not ask questions. If you do want the job, you better have a few good questions to ask. Since you did your research, you probably know a few things of interest about the company that were not brought up during the interview. Ask about them. For instance, "I read recently that the company has more than 100 employees. Are all of the employees at this location?" The point is, you did your homework on the company and you want them to know it.

Below are some possible questions the interviewer may ask (sample answers can be found in Appendix D):

➢ Where do you see yourself in five years?

➢ Do you have any difficulty working with others?

➢ Why do you want to work here?

➢ Why should we hire you?

➢ How well do you handle stress?

➢ What are your strengths?

- ➢ What are your weaknesses?

- ➢ What is your biggest pet peeve?

- ➢ What do you think of your previous employer?

- ➢ What did you like most about your last job?

- ➢ What did you like least about your last job?

- ➢ What was the last book you read? What did you learn?

- ➢ What starting salary do you expect?

- ➢ Do you prefer to work independently or with others?

- ➢ Where else have you applied?

- ➢ Why did you leave your last job?

- ➢ Why did you choose your major?

- ➢ How does your experience and education relate to this job?

- ➢ Describe a situation where you had to deal with a difficult customer.

- ➢ Give me an example where you tried something new and it worked.

- ➢ Give me an example where you tried something new and it failed.

Of course, some questions are illegal. Do not get too defensive right away. Sometimes the interviewer is not intentionally trying to ask these questions as a way to make a hiring decision; they may simply be trying to make small talk. Sometimes the person doing the interview is just as nervous as you are. If one of the illegal questions is asked, respond professionally. Either turn it back into a question, or respond by merely brushing across the answer and then mention how it will not affect your performance. Illegal questions include the following:

➢ Are you married?

➢ How old are you?

➢ What religion do you practice?

➢ Do you have children?

➢ Are you planning to have children?

A good response to one of the illegal questions may be, "I pride myself in separating my work life from my family responsibilities."

Next are some questions you may want to ask of the interviewer:

➢ When do you expect to make a decision on this position?

➢ Am I replacing someone who moved on from this position or is this a new position?

➢ What is the expected career track with this position?

There are also a few questions you should *not* ask of the interviewer:

➢ What type of salary can I expect?

➢ What kind of benefits do you offer?

➢ Do I get a discount on any of your products?

➢ Can I wear blue jeans on Fridays?

When the interviewer is ready to discuss salary and benefits they will bring it up. If they do not mention it don't worry about it until they call you back after the interview. If they offer you the job without having discussed any of the benefits, then you should bring them up before accepting their offer. You should also try to get an offer in writing. The easiest way to approach this topic is to ask your employer if the company will be sending you the offer in the mail. If not, then ask him or her to do so.

After the interview is over, you probably just want to go home and relax. Sorry. You are still not done. Now you get to go home and write your follow-up letter. This letter provides you the chance to thank the interviewer for his or her time. If you interviewed with more than one person you should write a follow-up letter to each one.

If you were paying close attention during the interview (or if you were taking notes), you may have noticed one or two particular concerns from each interviewer. You could address these concerns in your letter. For instance, if you heard, "Well, your grades look great, but you don't have a lot of experience," find a way to address that issue, such as mentioning your internship or how well you learn new things, and give an example.

The follow-up letter should be professional and polite. Keep it short and to the point. Its purpose is to show you are professional, address any last minute concerns, and most importantly, to remind the interviewer who you are. If the decision comes down to two or three close choices for the job, the one who sends a professional follow-up letter will most likely get the position. Take a look at the sample follow-up letter (Figure 3-1).

If you have not heard back from the interviewer for several days, you may want to make a follow-up telephone call. Simply remind the person who you are, "This is Anita Jobb. I interviewed with your company last Friday for the network programmer position." Next, tell them why you are calling, "I was calling to see if the position has been filled, or if there is any other information you may need from me." If the position was filled, you will be presenting yet another professional image of yourself. If something else opens up in the future, you may be remembered. If the position is still open, a professional phone call may be all it takes to show the interviewer you are the right person for the job.

Mr. Smith,

Thank you for giving me the opportunity to interview with you for the economist position last Thursday, November 10th. I am excited about the possibility of working for your company.

As mentioned in my interview, I will be graduating from The University of Maryland in May with a bachelor's degree in economics.

During the interview, you expressed some concern over my inexperience in the field of economics. While I have not been working full-time as a student, I did gain three months' experience as an intern for X-Stat where I was able to perform some economic forecasting. In addition, my overall academic achievements, especially in economics, demonstrate my ability to learn quickly and accomplish what is required to succeed.

If given the opportunity to work for your company, I will be able to use the experiences gained at X-Stat, as well as my knowledge of current economic modeling to help your company remain at the top of the industry.

If you have any additional questions for me, I can be reached at (301) 555-5555 or by email at kwerk@TheGraduatesGuide.com. Thank you again for your time and I look forward to hearing from you.

Sincerely,

Kent Werk

Figure 3-1: Sample Follow-up letter

If you do not get the job, be prepared to move on. Any form of rejection is difficult to handle. Just remember they were not rejecting you as a person, but something else such as your amount of experience or lack thereof. It's also possible the interviewer was just having a bad day when you interviewed or doesn't like your alma mater.

Anyway, don't be bitter. Another job with the same company may open up in the future. In some instances, where there is an interview committee, one or two of the members may have been really impressed by you, and they may still contact you in the near future if another opening becomes available in their department. If not, go to the next interview with the assumption this next company is the one that is fortunate enough to have the opportunity to meet you. Just don't tell them that.

After several interviews, if you still do not have any luck, you may want to take another look at your interviewing skills. Not getting a job does not necessarily mean you are a bad interviewer. However, it never hurts to have someone else take a look. Your career center at college may be willing to help you even if you already graduated. If not, get a relative to do a mock interview. You could even record the session to see how you present yourself and to listen to your voice. You should sit tall and still, but not stiff. Some hand movement is allowed, but don't start knocking things off the interviewer's desk while talking.

In the end, you just have to keep trying until you find the right job. Read back through the first three chapters and see if there is anywhere you could make improvements with your resume, cover letter, or interview techniques. Refer to Appendix B and check for the recommended books at your local library or bookstore. Good luck on your pursuit to find the perfect career!

You are now ready for your next action step.

Chapter 3 Action Step

1. Make sure you have an outfit appropriate for the interview. If you do not, get one or ask your parents for a little help.
2. Review the interview questions and answers in this chapter. Formulate your own answers to the questions and write them down so you can review before each interview. (But please do not take your notes into the interview with you.)
3. Do a mock interview. Either have a friend or family member perform the interview, or practice in front of the mirror. Trust me, if you can keep a straight face while interviewing yourself in front of a mirror, you're ready.

Chapter 3 Summary

❑   Look professional and confident during the interview.

❑   Err on the side of being too conservative.

❑   Be early.

❑   Do a dry run of the route to the interview at least the day before so you will not get lost.

❑   Bring extra copies of your resume with you.

❑   Ask good questions at the end of the interview.

❑   Write a thank-you letter to the interviewer(s).

❑   Practice interviewing with a friend, in front of a mirror, or with your career center at college.

Part II: The Basics

"You have to know where you want to go before you can get there. You have to know where you are now to figure out how."

4. **The Best Ways to "Bank" Your Money**

   ➢ Compare banks and credit unions

   ➢ Write a simple check

   ➢ Keep your checkbook balanced

5. **What Happened to My Paycheck?**

   ➢ Know what to expect from your first paycheck

   ➢ Choose the right amount to withhold from each pay

   ➢ Stretch your paycheck until it almost hurts

6. **Planning Life's Road Trip**

   ➢ Take a quick evaluation of your current situation

   ➢ Set your goals for the future

   ➢ Stay organized by filing the right papers

4

The Best Ways to "Bank" Your Money

Remember when you were just a kid and your piggy bank got full? Your parents told you it was time to open up a savings account. That way you could empty your piggy bank and start all over again. Years ago, banks gave out little booklets where they stamped your deposits and interest earned (called passbook savings accounts). In the years since, the banking industry has really matured. We now have more choices available to us than anyone could have imagined. Generally, you can do most of your "banking" at a bank, a savings & loan, or a credit union. A savings & loan is similar to a bank, but with fewer services. In general, I prefer credit unions. They tend to have lower fees, and they pay better rates on their savings accounts. Credit unions are generally easier to deal with than banks.

Most banks offer everything from financial investments, to certificates of deposit (CDs) and home mortgages. Banks tend to have higher fees and pay lower rates on their savings. Most banks also have minimum balance requirements on their accounts. If your account drops below the minimum amount, you will be charged a fee. You may be able to have the requirement waived if you have direct deposit from your employer. One of the advantages of banks is they normally have multiple branch locations. They may be located all over the city, the state, or even the country. For many people, having all of these available locations is most important.

Credit unions are very similar to banks in some aspects, but they are actually owned by the members. They usually exist for people with a common interest, such as working for the same union, or living in a specific community. For this reason, they tend to be more favorable to their members (or customers). Generally, the fees they charge are lower, the interest rates they pay are higher, and they do not require as large of a minimum balance, if any, in an account.

Of course, there are disadvantages of using credit unions. Most only have one or two branch locations (with some exceptions, such as state or federal employee credit unions) and the number of free ATM machines available tends to be very limited within a credit union network. Many of them do not offer first mortgages on your home, so you may still have to deal with a bank when you buy your first home.

When choosing between a bank and a credit union, you must decide what is important to you. If you run to the ATM every other day (a habit we'll discuss a little later on), you may prefer a bank with a large ATM network. If you tend to keep very low balances on your checking and savings accounts like most people, the credit union may be the better place to park your cash.

Whatever you decide, try to find a checking account with minimal or zero fees. There is nothing more painful than putting your money in a bank that charges you to do so. That would be like having a wallet or purse that charges you every time you open it. You'd probably just start keeping your money in your front pocket. Some banks even charge a fee for every check you use! Try to avoid these banks if at all possible. There are almost always better alternatives. Here are some tips on avoiding checking fees:

- Direct Deposit: Some banks waive account fees if your paycheck is direct deposited into your account. With a direct deposit, your money is wired directly into your account, so you don't have to wait in line to cash your paycheck. The downside is you still have to go to the bank (or an ATM) to get the cash.

- Average Daily Balance: If you do have a minimum balance requirement each month, using the average daily balance method is preferable. Some banks charge you a fee if your account balance falls below a certain amount any time during the month. If they use average daily balance, as long as the balance *averages* more than the minimum requirement, you won't pay a fee.

- Basic Checking: You may be able to find a basic checking account that offers no interest rate and no minimum balance, but only allows a select number of checks to be written and a select number of ATM withdrawals. If you use your ATM a lot, this won't work for you.

- Avoid ATM Fees: Find out what your bank's policy is for ATMs. Do they charge you each time you use one of their ATMs? What about an out-of-network ATM? How much do they charge per transaction? Also, see if there are only a limited number of free transactions per month. Be aware that some banks charge a fee to use your debit card. That's right; you pay for the privilege of spending your own money at the grocery store. Always look at the fine print.

Automated Teller Machines (ATMs)

A few points about ATMs. To begin, try not to use them more often than necessary. Not only is it difficult to track your account this way, but paying $4-$6 per transaction could really add up and crash your budget. Think about it, does it make sense to pay $5 just to get $40? It's your money to begin with. That is almost like paying a 150% annual interest rate, just to use your own money! Imagine you go to the ATM twice per week and get out $40 each time. If you pay a $5 fee for each transaction ($2 from your bank and $3 from the bank who owns the ATM), you would have paid $40 in one month just to withdraw a total of $320. That's more than 12% in one month out the window. Is 12% very much money? Ask yourself what you would do if your boss told you the company was going to have to cut your pay by 12%. That would be a $120 decrease for every $1,000 earned. It seems like a lot more money now, doesn't it?

Another key point is to keep your receipt. I am shocked at the number of ATM receipts lying around the ATM machines. You should keep your ATM receipt and put it with the rest of your receipts. Otherwise, you could really have a hard time keeping tabs on your account balance. While most machines only print the last few digits of your account, some print the first few digits on the receipt. A few digits may seem unimportant, but I say the less other people know about your bank accounts, the better.

Checks

I recommend purchasing carbon checks. Carbon checks have a carbon copy behind the real check so you have a record of who you paid, how much, and when. While I can view a scanned picture of the cashed check online at my bank, I still prefer the carbon checks. I never have to wonder if I paid someone, or what I used check #171 for. Besides, you are not going to be writing very many checks anyway.

Your bank will probably offer you fancy checks when you first open your account. That's fine if they are free, but once they are gone, try to buy no-frills checks. Remember, you are just giving them away (sometimes reluctantly). Your best bet is to not even purchase your checks from the bank. Yes, that's right, you don't have to buy your checks from the bank. Be sure to use a reputable check printing company and you could save a lot of money. You can even get fancier checks, if you must, at a much lower cost.

Even free checks won't do you any good if you don't know how to write a check. Figure 4-1 shows the fundamental features of a check and how to write one. If you make a minor mistake on your check (such as the wrong date) simply cross out the mistake, write-in the correction, and initial above the correction.

Remember to never sign a blank check! If you do, someone could fill in any dollar amount and cash it, especially if you drop or lose the blank check. That brings up another important point; you can stop payment on a check. There is usually a fee of between $20 and $35 to do this, but paying that may be better than losing hundreds of dollars or more.

There are other instances where you may want to stop payment on a check. Let's say you send a check to someone, because you made a purchase online. After more than a week the person claims they have not yet received your payment. You may want to send a new check or use another form of payment. In order to prevent them from cashing the original check (accidentally of course) if it does arrive a few days later, you should put a stop payment on it.

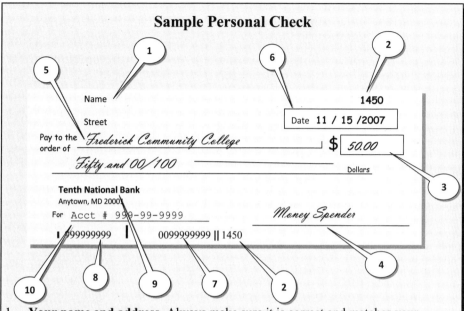

Figure 4-1: Sample Personal Check

1   **Your name and address**. Always make sure it is correct and matches your current identification card/driver's license.
2   **Check Number**. This is important when balancing your checkbook or resolving possible disputes. It can be found at the top and the bottom of the check.
3   **Amount**. Fill in the amount you are paying. Write so it is easily readable. Write the amount in words on the line. The numbers should be the same as in the box to the right. Put a line through any remaining space on the line.
4   **Your signature**. Sign as your name appears on the check (no nicknames).
5   **The Payee**. The person you are paying. You can also write a check to yourself in order to get money out of your own account.
6   **Date**. Make sure you use the proper date. Most checks are accepted for up to six months after the date.
7   **Account Number**. This is your checking account number.
8   **Routing Number**. You need this number for Direct Deposits and Automatic Withdraws (such as insurance payments, etc.).
9   **Name and address of your bank** (usually the main branch).
10 **Memo**. You can write a reminder so you know what the check is for (i.e., *birthday gift*). If you are making a payment, write the account number you are paying (i.e. for your phone bill, write the account number that appears on your phone bill). For credit cards, just write the last few digits, not the whole account.

Figure 4-1: Sample Personal Check

Once you begin using your checking account regularly, it becomes vital to know how much money is in your account. One purpose of keeping your checkbook balanced is to avoid bouncing checks (your account does not have enough cash in it to cover the amount on the check). Not only is this embarrassing, but you could run into real problems, such as having your car repossessed or losing your apartment, depending on the circumstances. At the very least your bank will charge a fee. One bounced check will not destroy you financially, but making a habit of it will. If you find you are having these problems, you really should keep a balanced checkbook.

The easiest way to balance your checkbook is to use a financial software program such as Quicken. You could enter your receipts once per week. Then, every month, when you get your bank statement, you can enter anything you missed and keep your account balanced. The goal here is just to avoid running out of money before the end of the month. As an added benefit, most software programs also have a feature that allows you to see where you spend your money (such as 40% in housing, 10% in taxes, 25% on entertainment, etc.).

If this doesn't sound like something you'll stick with, you can choose a bank or credit union that has your account details online. You can browse your account every few days and see which checks have cleared and which ones have not. Since you bought the carbon checks, you can easily see how much is yet to come out of your account. Plus, this is the easiest way to keep track of your ATM or bankcard withdraws. They usually post within three or four business days, while most banks post your transactions real-time.

Whatever method you decide to use to handle your banking needs, keep in mind there is a balance between time and cost. Don't let complacency get the better of you and end up paying the highest fees which just makes the bank richer. On the other hand don't cancel your weekend plans because you found the perfect bank, but you have to drive for three hours to get to it. If you find a moderate balance between convenience and cost you will not have to worry about your banking again for many years.

Just like any business banks exist to make money. While many of them try to help you with what they believe is in your best interest, they will usually only do so with what they have to offer. In other words, they may try to offer you the best loan program or the best checking account *they* have. However, another bank may actually offer a better program. Most banks are not going to tell you they do not have what you are looking for. You are expected to figure that out on your own. You have to go out and comparison-shop. Do not settle on a bank just because it is the one your parents used, or it is the one you used while you were in college. Your needs have changed and you may find another bank or credit union that will meet your needs at a lower cost.

If you plan to get a loan from your bank, refer to Chapter 10 where we discuss loans and debt. If you want to use your bank to establish a form of savings, investments, or even an IRA, you should definitely refer to Chapter 12 where we discuss savings and investments. Just because banks are larger and more impressive, doesn't mean you should trust them. After all, whose money do you think helped pay for all those large and impressive buildings?

Chapter 4 Action Step

Before you move on to the next chapter, I have an action step for you. Call or visit at least three banks or credit unions, even if you already have a bank. Compare their interest rates, their fees (late, overdraft, etc.) and their ATM policies. Also, compare how convenient they are for you, such as how close they are to your work and your home, and even their banking hours (some banks close by three o'clock).

Chapter 4 Summary

- Credit unions usually have lower fees and better customer service than banks.

- Banks generally have more locations, a larger ATM network and more products (such as mortgages) than credit unions.

- You should shop around to find the bank or credit union that best fits your overall needs.

- Be aware of how often you use the ATM and how much you are spending in fees just to get your own money from the bank.

- Never sign a blank check!

- You can balance your checkbook by hand or by using a software program. You can also track it online, but be aware of payments made by check or debit card that have not yet shown up on your account summary.

5
What Happened to My Paycheck?

Finally, we start to get into the good stuff. Let's talk about your paycheck. The first thing I realized after graduation was real life was nothing like I expected. Where was the company car or the corporate jet? Why did I still have to do my own laundry and clip coupons? Why could I barely even qualify to rent an apartment that I was too embarrassed to show my parents? I'll tell you why. It's called entry-level positions. You cannot expect to just graduate and become CEO of some company. Even with a college degree, most of us have to work our way up through the ranks. In fact, the average college graduate overestimates their starting salary by 44%. It takes a lot of work just to *remain* in the middle class. You start to appreciate all those times your dad complained about "leaving every light on in the house."

Aside from the first shocker that you are not quite worth a six-figure salary the day you graduate, you also experience the true costs of life. Rent is almost always more than one would expect. I remember when I first moved to the Washington, D.C. suburbs; I planned to spend $400 per month on rent. After all, my parents' house payment was only around $300. Then, my being the financial wizard that I was, I decided to cushion my budget to allow for a whopping $500 for rent. So, I took a job that paid low, but had potential. The only problem was the apartments I wanted to rent were well over $1,000 per month! Not only were they too expensive, I couldn't even "qualify" for them anyway. After looking at various apartments (if you can even call them that) that cost less than $1,000 per month, I finally found one that was *just* $620 per month and *only* 45 minutes away from my job. So much for financial independence.

Then came the best part. I got my first paycheck! Well, clearly there must have been some mistake. After all, I did the math and unless they were going to give me an extra paycheck every month, there was no way those numbers even resembled the ones we talked about in the interview. I mean, I could have made more money sitting outside the subway station holding a can and a "Will work for food" sign!

If you look at a typical pay stub it will probably look something like Figure 5-1. Of course the numbers will be different, but I believe it fairly represents what you will see.

Business Name						Check No:	A00001		
Business Address						Check Date:	02/07/xx		
						Period Ending:	02/01/xx		

Kent Werk					TAX ADJUSTMENTS			
123 Job Lane		Salary:	26,000.00		FED:	ST:		
Greenville, NC 27858		SSN:	123-45-6789		LOCAL:			

HOURS AND EARNINGS					TAXES AND DEDUCTIONS			OTHER	
		Current		YTD			Current	YTD	
Description	Hours	Earnings	Hours	Earnings	Description		Amount	Amount	Vac Balance 18.00
									Sick Balance 23.00
Regular	80.00	1000.00	240.00	3000.00		**PRE-TAX**			Retire Match 150.00
					Retirement		100.00	300.00	
					Health Ins		45.00	135.00	
					FSA		20.00	60.00	
						AFTER-TAX			
					Social Sec.		62.00	186.00	
					Medicare		14.50	43.50	
					Fed		95.60	286.80	
					State		41.75	125.25	
					Life		5.00	15.00	

	GROSS	OTHER	TAXABLE	LESS TAXES	LESS DEDUCTIONS	NET PAY
Current	1000.00		835.00	213.85	170.00	616.15
YTD	3000.00		2505.00	641.55	510.00	1848.45

Figure 5-1: Sample Pay Stub

When I started my first job after college, there was apparently a bit of miscommunication at the interview and the new employee orientation. You see, I thought they were actually going to *pay* me to work for them! The truth is, they overemphasized how much I would make my first year, but they underemphasized that nearly 10% of the promised amount would be made at the end of the year in the form of a bonus. That brings up a serious cash flow issue (which will be discussed in Chapter 6). See, I could not tell my landlord that I would pay him most of the rent during the year and pay him a 10% bonus amount at the end of the year. I had to spread my payments out evenly every month. So, the low pay and the high rent meant I only kept that job for about two months before I moved on.

But here is the real kicker. Even going by the real amount I should have been making every pay, I only saw about 65% of that. That's right, for every $100 earned; I only got to see about $65. So where did it go? There are actually several places your money goes once you get paid. It's depressing in a way, but at least you can be better prepared and you can budget accordingly.

Let's talk about all of the different items listed on the check.

Fed Tax: I think this one is pretty simple. This is the federal tax you pay from each check.

State Tax: Again, a basic concept. This would be the state tax you pay. Usually you will not find a separate locality pay, but it does happen occasionally. Your locality is usually a city such as Baltimore City.

Social Security/FICA: This is your social security tax. On some paystubs it is labeled FICA and on others it is labeled Social Security. You pay 6.2% of your salary to FICA. It stands for Federal Insurance Contribution Act. Don't feel too bad though, because your employer contributes an additional 6.2% into FICA also, so the tax is really 12.4% for social security, but only half of that is actually pulled away from your earnings.

Med: You have probably heard of Medicare. This is the system that helps the elderly with medical expenses. You pay 1.45% towards Medicare. Your employer matches the same amount.

Health: Your health insurance may be taken from your paycheck either pre-tax or post-tax. Either way it gets taken out of the gross amount and makes your net amount smaller. For most people, their employer actually pays a much larger share of the health insurance cost than they do.

Life: Your employer may offer a life insurance policy. The policy is usually for a small amount, such as two times your annual salary.

Retirement: There are several categories available here. This could be the amount you choose to contribute (such as a 401(k)), or perhaps your employer automatically deducts a certain percentage and places it into an account for you.

FSA: The Flexible Spending Account is an amount you choose to set aside for medical costs. We will discuss the FSA in Chapter 13.

ESOP: The Employee Stock Ownership Plan is a benefit you signed up for. If you did not, go and speak to someone in your human resource department. The ESOP is money taken from your paycheck and used to purchase company stock. Sometimes the company will match a portion of your ESOP contribution, but they do not have to. An ESOP is another form of savings.

There may be others, depending on what your employer offers in the form of benefits. You may also have stock options or other such benefits that show up on your pay stub. I have given you the most common deductions that decrease your gross pay.

That brings up another point. There are two types of pay that really matter: Gross pay and net pay. Gross pay is actually the larger of the two. Your gross pay is what you make before taxes. If you are an hourly employee, your gross pay is simply your hourly rate multiplied by the number of hours you worked. For a salaried employee, your gross pay is your annual salary divided by the number of paychecks you receive in a year (typically 26). If this is not the case, you should speak with someone in personnel and find out why.

Net pay is the one that tells you what's left over after all of the deductions previously discussed. You start with gross pay, then taxes are taken out, and insurance, retirement, and so forth. That's why your net pay is always so much smaller than your gross pay. As a quick estimate, you can assume your net pay will be between 60% and 70% of your gross pay, depending on how much your insurance costs, and how much you contribute towards retirement, etc. Think of it this way. If you had a fish aquarium with ten fish, that's the gross amount. But, when you use the net to scoop them out, you may only get six or seven of the fish in your first swoop, thus you *netted* six or seven fish. That's like net pay; it's the amount you *net* from the total.

To calculate how much is taken from your paycheck for taxes your employer uses a formula. Each state is different, but federal taxes use the same type of formula. When you first get hired you fill out a bunch of paperwork. One of the forms you sign is called your W-4. This form determines how many exemptions you take. When you first start out, you should probably be claiming zero exemptions. If your parents are still claiming you as a deduction (which they may do if you just graduated this year) you definitely want to claim zero exemptions in order to avoid owing any more tax than necessary next April.

For each exemption you take, the government basically "exempts" a certain portion of your paycheck from being taxed, so the more exemptions you take, the less that comes out of each paycheck. However, at the end of the year (actually when you file your taxes by April 15th) your entire tax liability is computed based on your income for the year. So if you took too many exemptions and did not have enough taxes taken out of each paycheck, you will owe the difference at the end of the year.

In other words, the number of exemptions you claim on your W-4 does not affect the total amount of taxes you will pay by the time you file in April; it only affects how much you pay each week. See Figure 5-2 for a table that illustrates how much tax is withheld each paycheck. See Figure 5-3 for an example of how the formula works on a paycheck (the numbers change each year because tax brackets adjust slightly to account for inflation).

Keep in mind how you are taxed throughout the year does not really affect the total amount of taxes you owe for the year. Simply stated, you either pay too much as you go along, and get money back when you file the following year, or you pay too little from each paycheck and you owe money when you file the following year. Occasionally you may pay exactly what you owe, but usually you'll be off by at least a few dollars in either direction. We'll discuss taxes in more detail in Chapter 14.

Bi-weekly Payroll Period (every two weeks)
for a Single Person (or Head of Household)
(For Tax Year 2010)

If the amount of wages
(after subtracting   The amount of income tax
withholding allowance) is: to withhold is:

Over:	But not over:				of excess over:
$233	.............$401	.........10%	....	....	.................$233
$401	.........$1,387	...........$16.80	plus	15%	.................$401
$1,387	.........$2,604	........$164.70	plus	25%	..............$1,387
$2,604	.........$3,248	........$468.95	plus	27%	..............$2,604
$3,248	.........$3,373	........$642.83	plus	30%	..............$3,248
$3,373	.........$6,688	........$680.33	plus	28%	..............$3,373
$6,688	........$14,450	......$1,608.53	plus	33%	..............$6,688
$14,450	....	......$4,169.99	plus	35%	............$14,450

Note: If the amount of wages is below $233, no tax is withheld.

Figure 5-2: Bi-weekly Payroll Withholding Table

Let's look at an example of how your employer deducts from your paycheck. Assume you earn $26,000 per year and are paid every two weeks (bi-weekly).

1	Gross Earnings on each paycheck	$1,000.00
2	Assume you deduct $165.00 for your 401(k), health insurance, and FSA, and take zero exemptions	-165.00
3	Your taxable income becomes:	$ 835.00
4	According to Figure 5-2, your withholdings will be $16.80 plus 15% of the amount over $401 (row 5):	$16.80
5	Since your taxable income is $835, you take $835 minus $401 = $434. You will pay $16.80 (row 4) plus 15% of $434 which is $65.10 (.15 x $434 = $65.10)	65.10
6	Your federal tax withholding will total $81.90 ($16.80 plus $65.10 = $81.90)	-81.90
7	After subtracting your deductions and your federal taxes your paycheck will be reduced to:	$ 753.10

Of course you will also pay state, Social Security, and Medicare taxes. Refer to the paycheck example (Figure 5-1) to see how your paycheck might end up.

Figure 5-3: Example Calculating Bi-weekly Payroll Withholding

Stretching Your Paycheck

I know what you are thinking. I can't believe I went through four years of academic torture just to come out on the other side and have to watch where and how I spend my money!

Remember those points I made in the "Before You Begin" section? (You did read that section, right?) The first point was your parents have more money than you. In many cases your parents *make* more money than you, especially when you first start out. Don't feel too bad, because you can't forget point number three; your parents have been working for more than 20 years.

Even if they don't make more than you, they probably still have more money than you. Here is why. For one, there's inflation. My parents had a house payment of around $300 because they bought their home many years ago. When I tried to find an apartment, I was paying more than twice that amount. My townhouse cost about four times what my parents paid for their home! You see, I would have to make a lot more than them just to break even after rent (or mortgage).

Another reason your parents have more money than you is because they have had several years to save. That's right, they have since paid off their college loans (if they had any), and hopefully their other debts as well. They may have even paid off their mortgage. (If not, you may want to let them read the chapter on loans and debt. Make your parents proud and show them how all the money they spent on your education has paid off.)

A third reason your parents have more money than you... and I hate to admit it... is because they are smarter than you. Remember I am still only talking about money here. Just remember who it was that always left the television on and the lights on and the door open. Was it your dad? No, he was going around closing doors and turning off lights (all the while grumbling, I'm sure).

Your parents have learned through the years how to make their dollars go further (they had to when they had you). Usually, they do not even have to think about it anymore, it just comes naturally. After all, you weren't "raised in a barn." I do have two pieces of good news. First, you don't have to *admit* your parents are smarter than you. Second, after you finish this book, you'll be smarter than them! That's right; you're going to be twenty years ahead of your time in terms of financial knowledge.

Ways to Stretch Your Money

There are a lot of things you could do to make your paycheck stretch further. You may think they are all going to be painful, but they are not. Keep in mind there are an unlimited number of ways you could spend your money, but unfortunately you only earn a limited amount. The point is you will have to make choices. Figure out what is important to you and don't let anything get in your way of achieving it. Usually we sacrifice the big, important things for the small, insignificant ones. Look at the ideas that follow for ways to stretch your budget.

Save on Food

➢ Skip the name brand foods, and get the store brands. The same companies that make the name brands usually make the generic ones as well, but they are not spending money in advertising costs and fancy packaging. I have found that cheap ketchup and mayonnaise just don't work though.

➢ Watch for sales. Look at the store ads in the newspaper (or online). If you don't really need something this week, just wait and see if it comes on sale the next week. Don't be afraid to look at more than one grocery store. You'll quickly learn where the better deals are.

➢ Make a list of things you need and only buy what is on the list. Most grocery carts are full of things that were not on the list in the first place. Nothing is worse than food going to waste when you are on a tight budget.

➢ Brown bag it. If you pack a lunch every day instead of dining out, you could save more than $1,200 per year. Also, you could actually use left over grocery bags (the plastic ones) instead of buying the brown lunch bags.

➢ Clip coupons. Too much of a headache? Just do it the easy way. Flip through the Sunday ads, and only clip coupons that are at least 50 cents and only for those products you always purchase, such as your favorite brand of coffee, cereal, peanut butter, etc. Also look for food coupons from pizza places, or any of the restaurants you always end up going to on Friday nights (and Saturdays, and Tuesdays). Do not use coupons just because you have them. Only use them to buy the things you were already going to purchase anyway.

➤ Skip the appetizers. Most restaurants charge at least $5-$7 for an appetizer. Unless you are splitting with friends, they are usually just a waste of money. Not only do they tend to be unhealthy (think cheese, plus carbs, plus grease), but they also keep you from finishing your $15-$20 meal.

Curb Some Habits

➤ Make your own coffee in the morning (assuming you drink coffee). Don't pay $2 or $3 per day for coffee, when you could make it for just cents a day. At just $3 per workday, you are spending more than $700 per year on coffee.

➤ If you smoke, then quit. I know it is not that simple but do what you have to do to quit smoking. How can you complain about never having any money when you are spending more than $50 a month on a bad habit? Think about it.

➤ Don't make any large purchases until you have thought about it for at least 24 hours. You've made it this long without it, so what is another day? If you can, wait a whole week. This really works. Think about how many things you have that you just don't use. By waiting a couple of days, you may forget about it or realize you really don't need it.

➤ Remember, you do not have to be the first. Yes, we all like the latest and newest gadget, but don't purchase items as soon as they come out. Wait a few months and the price will drop significantly. Look at Blue-ray DVD players. When they first became popular, they were priced at more than $500. Even after just a few months, they were priced below $400. About a year later you could get a better one for $300. Now they are even less expensive. Let your buddies spend their money. You can get the same model a few months later much cheaper.

Save at Home

➤ Take a look at your telephone bill(s). Do you need call waiting? Do you use all 9,000 minutes on your cell phone? Do you always go over your minutes? There is money to be saved here.

➤ How much time do you really have to watch television? Do you watch 99 channels, or do you watch five of them? How often do you watch the premium channels? Remember, this is about choices. Would you rather spend your money watching television at home, or would you rather spend another night out at the movies?

➤ Don't use so much electricity when you are asleep. You should adjust your thermostat when you go to bed so you are using your heating/cooling less. In fact, you could adjust it before you go to work. The best bet is to get a programmable thermostat (if your landlord will allow it) and set it to change accordingly. That way your house could still be comfortable by the time you get home from work.

There are, of course, entire books devoted to saving money and spending less. Hopefully I have given you a few ideas you can use. The important thing to remember is you may struggle a bit in the beginning, but you can look forward to moving up through the ranks. If you are one of the fortunate ones who make more money than you can handle right after college, you should still try to be conservative with your spending. You may want to refer to Chapters 10 and 11 about getting out of debt. If you do not have any debt, then definitely look into Chapter 12 to learn the best strategies for saving.

Since we are talking about your paycheck in this chapter, now is a good time to mention one very important tip. Look over your entire pay stub and check for mistakes. I know you are already scanning every little deduction hoping to find a mistake. Chances are everything will be accurate, but if you have any questions, ask someone in Human Resources to explain the deduction. Don't be surprised if they are unsure about certain items. Perhaps they too can learn something new from your question.

Don't get too caught up just in the dollars. Make sure your social security number is right. I have heard horror stories about people who work for several years, and all of their social security benefits went to someone else, because they had the wrong social security number on their pay stub. In fact, something similar happened in my household. Fortunately we caught the mistake and had it corrected before it was too late. It only takes one digit to make the difference. If there is a mistake, have it corrected immediately. Assuming it is your first paycheck no harm was done. If you have been working for a while you may want to follow up with it and make sure you are credited for all of your contributions to social security, including those made before you discovered the mistake.

Chapter 5 Action Step

How would you like an easy action step? Okay, all you have to do is look over your entire pay stub and check for mistakes. That's it. I want to make sure you understand everything on your check. Make sure the social security number is correct, the vacation hours are correct, etc. If there is any part of your check you do not understand, talk to your Human Resources department. It is better to catch something early than to regret it later.

Chapter 5 Summary

- Gross pay is the larger number on your paycheck. It is what you actually earned before any deductions were taken out.

- Net pay is what is left over in your paycheck after all of your deductions are taken.

- Expect to 'net' between 60% and 70% of your salary, after taxes, insurance, retirement, etc. are taken out.

- Adjusting your withholdings only slightly changes the amount of each paycheck. It does not affect the total amount of taxes you will owe for the year.

- In order to make your money last longer you can curb some of your spending habits or look for other ways to cut back on wasted expenses.

6
Planning Life's Road Trip

Y ou've probably heard the saying, "Nobody plans to fail, but they fail to plan," so I promise I won't mention it. If you set zero goals for yourself, that is exactly how many you will achieve. This is not about getting in touch with your inner self or anything, it is just common sense planning.

There are three basic questions to ask yourself in order to plan:

1. Where am I? You need to assess your current financial and life situations.
2. Where do I want to go? You should plan for major financial decisions such as retirement, as well as minor ones, such as vacation.
3. How do I want to get there? You have many options available. The more knowledge you have, the better you can make the decisions that will be right for you.

These three questions are essential to any type of planning. Just think of this plan as your financial road map (or your GPS navigator, if you prefer). If you were planning a trip, you obviously need to know your starting point. A trip to the Grand Canyon is completely different if you were coming from Washington, D.C. as opposed to Denver, Colorado. You also need to know where you are going; otherwise you won't get there. Finally, you have to plot your course. Do you take the quickest route, the shortest route, or the scenic route? That's what we are going to explore.

Where Am I Now?

The best way to find out where you are is to ask some serious questions. Are you married or single? Are you planning to have children in the near future? Do you rent, own, or live with your parents? Are you in a stable job? Do you like it? These are the types of questions you need to ask in order to figure where you are in your personal and financial life.

Getting Organized

"I'm sure I didn't throw it away. It has to be around here somewhere..." Does that sound familiar? I know it's not the most fun after-work activity, but it is important we keep our most important papers safe. Okay, we also have to be able to *find* them. I know plenty of people that have their mortgage deed in a safe place, somewhere in the bedroom... or was that in the attic? In an emergency situation (need to file a claim on your car insurance) or during a dispute ("I know my credit card balance was not *that* high!") you need to be able to easily find your documents.

The easiest way to keep all of your important papers together and readily available is to organize them in a file cabinet. Just get several manila folders and label them according to their category. Below is a list of common files to keep:

- Bank Account
- Auto
- Insurance
- Retirement
- Other Investments
- Pay Stubs
- House / Rent
- Taxes
- Warranties
- Utilities
- Phone
- Credit Card(s)
- Loan(s)
- Pet(s)
- School/Child Care

Another option is to get a three ring binder with pocket inserts and keep your documents in there. That way you can move all of your files together if you need them.

Once you create your files, you may wonder how long to keep everything. Eventually the folders will get full and then you'll stop using them, and then you can't find anything... As a general rule, you should keep everything for one full year. Once you get a year-end statement that agrees with your records, throw out the monthly statements. Otherwise, always have the prior 12 months handy. You should keep your tax records for seven years, since the IRS can still come after you for up to seven years. Any records for your home (if you own one) should be kept until you sell it and file your taxes. When you pay off your car loan, you will receive a document that says so. Keep it until you sell your car. You should also have at least 12 months worth of pay stubs, even if you have your year-end statement. Many banks and mortgage companies are interested in seeing a few of the actual pay stubs if you apply for a loan.

In a safer location you should keep the following:
- Birth Certificates
- Passport
- Social Security Card (never carry this in your wallet)
- Marriage certificate
- Adoption papers
- Wills/Trust

Basically, anything that could seriously cause you hardship should it be lost, stolen, or destroyed, should be kept in a fire proof safe at home or in a safety deposit box. One exception is that wills should not be kept in a safety deposit box, because the person who dies may be the only one who has access to that box. It is better to keep your will with your attorney or in a fireproof safe at home. You can also keep a *copy* of it in the safety deposit box or even with your other important files.

In a separate file, you may want to keep a bill organizer. Bill organizers can be purchased at low cost at almost any office store. You can organize your bills by due date or by keeping all the payment stubs of each kind together and keep your bills that are still due in another folder. You can also use one of those desktop organizers that have at least 31 slots. That way you put the bill in whichever slot corresponds to the due date (or the date you want to send the payment). I like to keep a chart that lists all of my bills and their due dates. That way each month when I pay them, I place a checkmark in that month's column. Just try to find whatever method keeps you from missing your payment due dates.

Of course the easiest way to make sure you pay all of your bills on time is to pay them all online. It is still important to keep track of when they are due because of that pesky cash flow issue. It is one thing to set up an automatic withdrawal every month on the right date. It is quite another thing to make sure you have enough money in your account to actually cover the expense.

Receipts may be one of the biggest pains you'll deal with when you try to stay organized. Unless you use your receipts to track your spending, you can just throw away any receipt from a purchase made in cash, such as gas, groceries, or dinner. If you paid by credit card, make sure your account number does not appear on the receipt. If it does, you should shred it.

You do need to keep your warranty information when you make a purchase. The easiest way is to make one of your files for warranties and put all of the information in this file. You could also use a manila folder to keep the receipts for those items so they won't get lost. Believe me, when your surround sound system breaks (the one you paid *way* too much money for) you'll be happy you can find your warranty information right away. Once a warranty expires, just toss the receipt. If you really want to be organized, keep a sheet of paper in the envelope (or just write on the outside of the envelope) and list the name of the item and the date of expiration (Washer & Dryer: June 5, 2012). You can always go back and clean out the outdated receipts when you get free time. Whatever you do, be consistent. Don't put half of your warranty receipts in one place and do something different with the rest. Just pick a system and stick with it.

I will be the first to point out that having a cluttered desk can lead to a cluttered life. The opposite is also true. Trust me; I am the authority on messy desks. When my desk is clean and everything is organized, I'm ready to go. I'm ready to be productive! It's so invigorating to actually see the wood grain. ("You were right, my desk *is* maple.") Of course the other option is to just move your laptop computer somewhere clean (I don't think my wife has caught on to me yet). When everything is messy on the other hand, I tend to be more tired. I can get overwhelmed just staring at my desk. There isn't enough room to work, and I can't really find anything. Two good rules to remember (courtesy of my wife, who is much more organized than I am):

1.   Only touch each piece of paper once. In other words, get it out of your inbox and either file it or take care of it.
2.   As soon as you are done with something, put it away.

Identity theft is also a major concern, and good record keeping can help you avoid, or minimize the damage from, identity theft. By keeping good records, such as bank and credit card statements, you can easily identify unauthorized account activity (that sounds very attorney-like, doesn't it?). Below are a few common safety precautions to keep in mind:

➢ Never carry your social security card in your wallet – If a thief gets your driver's license *and* social security card, you could be in serious trouble.

➢ Do not have your social security number printed on your checks.

➢ Make a list of everything you keep in your wallet (or purse) – You need the names, telephone numbers, and account numbers from each card. Better yet, photocopy everything front and back. Keep these copies wherever you file your other records.

➢ Do not just throw away credit card solicitations, but shred them or burn them. You can recycle everything but the part that has any of your personal information.

➢ You can contact the major credit bureaus and request that no new accounts be open in your name without written consent. See Appendix E for contact information.

Do the Math

Now that you have all of your papers and such together, you can find out what your current financial situation is. Your first step is to calculate your net worth. Sadly, it is probably negative at this point in your life. If not, consider yourself either lucky or financially smart. Most people have college loans, car loans and credit card debt to contend with. Add that to the fact that at this point in your life you do not own much of anything and you have the perfect formula for a negative net worth.

I shouldn't get too far ahead of myself here. You need to know how to calculate your net worth. Basically, add up everything you own. It doesn't matter how much you paid, but how much it would be worth if you were to sell it. That $500 sofa is probably only worth about $200 once it is a year old. Your car has also depreciated (decreased in value).

Once you get that total, add up everything you owe. Look at all of your credit cards, car loans and college loans. Add all of your debt, then subtract that from what you own. That is your net worth. You should look for ways to increase your net worth (not by using "creative accounting," but by increasing assets and decreasing debts).

It would also be useful to look at all of your other monthly payments. Just to get an idea of how much it costs you to live, you should list all of your bills, including your utilities and rent, as well as how much you spend at the grocery store and dining out. Looking at all of these items should give you a good picture of where you are today.

Use the chart (Figure 6-1) to record all of your expenses, or at least an estimate. If you are preparing to move out on your own, list what you expect you will be paying once you get your own place. This chart could help you in several ways. First, you can see what your total monthly payments will be. Second, you will be able to see where most of your money goes (entertainment, dining out, etc.). Finally, you can use that information to determine if there are areas where you need to reduce spending. If you want to know what percentage of your expenditures is going to which category, simply divide any expenditure by your monthly income. For instance, if you spend $200 per month on your car payment, and you earn $800 per month, you spend $200/$800 = .25 = 25% of your income on your car payment alone.

Where Do I Want to Go?

Now you have to ask yourself where you want to go. Do you plan to retire in another 30 years? Another 20? Are you planning to get married and have children? How many children do you want to have? Do you want to buy a house or continue to rent? Basically, your task here is to just ask questions of yourself. You want to know what it is you want for yourself out of life. Here is a good place to set all of your goals.

To separate your priorities, you need to write down your goals. But break them into three segments, short-term, medium-term and long-term. Your short-term goals should be things you want within the next year. These may include getting a new television or a few new outfits for work. Your medium-term goals should be the things you will want within the next one to five years such as purchasing a new car or buying a home. Your long-term goals are what you want five or more years into the future. You should include retirement, maybe funding a child's college education and perhaps purchasing a vacation home. Your goals do not have to be things you will buy. You may have a goal of moving to the beach within three years, or starting a family in the next two.

Whatever it is you want to do with your life can be listed as a goal. Keeping things in this perspective will help you focus as you get out of bed every morning, fight with traffic and wonder why you can't just go back to college and let your parents send you money.

None of these goals have to be set in stone, but you will at least have an idea of what your priorities are. After you have made your list, go back through and decide if these are really the things that are important to you. If so, then number them in order of importance.

Housing		**Insurance**	
Mortgage/Rent		Car	
Utilities		House	
Furnishings		Medical	
Transportation		**Debt**	
Car 1		Credit	
Car 2		Loans	
Maintenance		Extra	
Gas		**Miscellaneous**	
Other		**Child Care**	
Food/Groceries		Day Care	
Entertainment		School	
Dining Out		Babysitting	
Activities		**Pets**	
Vacation		**Gifts**	
Clothing		Major Holidays	
Clothes		Tithes/Offerings	
Dry Cleaning		Other	
Savings		**Taxes**	
Regular Savings		Federal	
Long-Term		State & Local	
Retirement		FICA	

Figure 6-1: Record of Expenses

How Do I Want to Get There?

Now that you have an idea of what you want out of life, you have to decide how you want to go about getting there. Are you willing to work longer hours to make more money so you can retire early? Would you prefer to delay all of your goals if you can find a job that does not pay as well, but is exactly the type of work you are looking for? We are so fortunate to have so many choices in life. Unfortunately, it is possible to make the wrong ones. Your best bet is to prioritize your goals and decide what is most important to you. As you go through life you may experience several detours. As long as you always know what it is you want to do and how you want to get there you will be able to adjust to all of these little detours without setting yourself back.

At this point you may want to consider speaking with a financial planner. You will be looking at your retirement plans through work (if you are working) and see if you are currently on pace to meet your goals. Also, using the rest of the information in this book you should be able to look at alternative ways to save money and invest and get out of debt quickly so you can start working towards all of your major life goals.

Hopefully you were able to see where I was going with my analogy of how planning your future is similar to planning a road trip. If you didn't pick up on it, don't worry about it because the rest of the book isn't nearly so deep. Just remember all of the key points about getting organized, and make your list of goals. From there you can decide what changes or sacrifices you are willing to make to reach those goals, or perhaps you may decide some of your goals are not really as important to you after all.

Chapter 6 Action Step

You have two small action steps for this chapter. First, set up some sort of filing system, either with notebooks or manila folders or whatever. Create categories like the ones mentioned earlier in the chapter. You should sort through the papers you have scattered about now and put them in the proper file. Try to use this system as new documents come in, and clean it out once per year. Your second action step is to write down or photocopy the information for everything in your wallet. If something gets lost or stolen this small step could save you hours of trouble. You might also save hundreds of dollars, depending on the fate of your credit and debit cards.

It's that simple. A little bit of time devoted to being organized, and you will save a lot of time, and headaches, later.

Chapter 6 Summary

❑ Keeping all of your financial papers organized is an essential part of your overall financial health.

❑ In order to plan you have to first find out where you are. That is why it is essential to add up your assets and your debts and see what your current situation is. You should also create a budget to get an idea of where you are spending your income.

❑ Set your short-term and long-term goals now so you can plan where you want to go.

❑ Once you know what you want, you can decide how you want to get there. Knowing what your options are will make your decision much easier.

Part III: On Your Own

"We do a great job providing education to support students through their four years of college, but we sometimes fail to provide the education to support them through their next ten."

7. **Your First Apartment: Meals Not Included**

   ➤ Know where to look to find the right apartment

   ➤ Know your rights as a tenant

   ➤ Use a few "tricks" to help you save time and money

8. **I Work, Therefore I Drive**

   ➤ Decide whether to buy, lease, or just walk to work

   ➤ Prepare for the sales person before you walk onto the lot

   ➤ Maintain your car to keep it problem free

9. **Home Sweet Home of Your Own**

   ➤ Calculate your mortgage costs

   ➤ Know what to look for when preparing to buy a home

   ➤ Maintain your home (and your appliances) to save money over time

7

Your First Apartment: Meals Not Included

Finding an apartment can be a big pain. If you are in an area with a tight housing market (more people than places), it gets even worse. If you have already looked for an apartment, and staying with your parents for a while is not an option, I know what you are thinking. I can't get a job and go to work unless I have a place to stay. I can't find a place to stay unless I have a job to make money. Well, it gets a little worse. You can't get a place to stay to get the job to make the money unless you already have money available for the security deposit! I know it's not fair, but that's what we get to deal with starting out after college. My security deposit was the second largest transaction on my credit card when I was starting out. I wasn't happy.

Most apartments require a security deposit of at least $250. Sometimes, the deposit could be as large as two months' rent. Part of the problem could be your virtually nonexistent credit history. Oh yeah, did I forget to mention most apartment complexes check your credit? Even some landlords check your credit and rental history. They may also ask for recommendations from your previous landlord(s). I hope you didn't treat your last apartment like a rock star's hotel room.

In most major metropolitan areas you will be able to find apartment guides. They are readily available for free at grocery stores, usually near the exits. These guides are useful for choosing from the large apartment complexes in the area. They are usually arranged by location, which is great if you know where you do and don't want to stay. You can make a list of the places that interest you and call to see if they have any available apartments.

You can also use the Internet to search for apartments. One popular site is *www.rent.com*. You can search based on your own criteria (such as pool, pets, etc.). Once you find a few in your price range, you should contact them and arrange for a walkthrough. You can also find other interesting information on this site such as moving tips and articles. There are other sites as well including Craig's List. You can find them using a search engine, or you can visit the city's website. Most cities have a community information website with links to area businesses, including apartment complexes.

A third option is to look through the local newspaper. If you already live in the area, just pick up a local paper and browse the classifieds. Most apartment listings will be in the Saturday or Sunday editions, but Wednesdays are also popular. You can also browse the classifieds online.

If you end up renting from an individual, make sure you read the contract carefully before signing anything and handing over any money. Actually, that holds true for any contract. Be especially careful if you are not renting from an apartment complex or through a real estate agent.

Speaking of real estate agents, you may want to consider using one to help you find an apartment. Many people think real estate agents are only for buying and selling homes. In many cases, landlords will list their property through a real estate agency to save them the hassle of trying to find a tenant and showing them the property. The agent makes some money (less than if they sold the property, but without nearly as much effort) and the landlord gets a new tenant without doing much work. Just like buying a home, you do not pay the real estate agent. Their commission comes from the homeowner. In a real tight housing market it may be difficult to find any agents willing to deal with rentals. In many cases the newer, less experienced agents work with renters. Nonetheless, the best apartment we ever rented was located with the help of a real estate agent.

Knowing Your Rights as a Tenant

Once you think you have found the ideal apartment, start looking very carefully at the lease contract. How long are you locking yourself in? Some contracts are six months, others are for one year, and some are for 18 months or even two years. You also want to find out how long of a notice you have to give before you leave. In some cases you have to notify your landlord two months before the end of the lease if you do not want to renew it. Landlords usually reserve the right to show your apartment to new prospective renters during the final thirty days of your lease. If you don't know what will happen 12 months from now, you may want to find out if you can rent month-to-month. Some contracts allow this option after you have been in the apartment for one full year, but you still need to give them enough notice (such as 30 or 60 days) before you do finally move out.

What happens if you get transferred or lose your job? What if your dream home becomes available just six months into your 12-month lease? You should find out what the penalties are for breaking your lease. Some contracts try to obligate you for the entire annual rental amount. Most will stipulate that you can break your lease for a fee, but you are still responsible for the rent until another tenant is found. That could be bad if no one else comes along and takes over your lease. Other contracts simply charge you a larger fee, such as one month's rent, and allow you to break the lease at any time.

Be sure there are not any stipulations you absolutely cannot live with that are in the contract. If you have any pets, make sure they are welcome in your apartment. In many cases you have to pay an additional pet fee, such as $25 extra per month, or an extra $250 pet security deposit, or both. Decide if your pets are really worth all of that (just kidding!). Also, you may not be able to have more than a certain number of visitors, or visitors after a certain hour. Yes, it really can be more restrictive than a college dorm at times. That's because the landlord can't just go to your parents if there are problems (unless they cosign the lease). Just look for anything in the contract that really annoys you. You can try to negotiate. Most landlords use a standard form. They may be willing to make small changes if you seem like a trustworthy tenant (use the same charm that worked for you in the job interview).

As for specific tenant rights, almost every state has resources available. You can check on the Internet for tenant rights organizations, most of which are non-profits or government sponsored organizations to help you with any landlord disputes. Many of them also offer general guidelines and tips. Since each state has its own set of rules, and many cities also have their own specific guidelines, I won't try to list them here. In Appendix C, I have listed several websites you can browse for specific tenant rights. Below is a list of some common rights that usually apply no matter where you live.

➤ Your landlord must give you "reasonable" notice before entering your apartment. In other words, he can't just let himself in while you are in the shower. Usually the landlord is required to give 24 hours notice. Be sure to check your lease.

> ➤ You cannot be denied housing based on race, color, sex, religion, disability, family status, or national origin. This is federal law (The Fair Housing Act).

> ➤ Your dwelling must be habitable and in compliance with local health codes. In other words, your apartment cannot be falling apart or unsanitary. It must also provide adequate heat, electricity and water (assuming you pay your utility bills on time).

> ➤ Your landlord must complete repairs and maintenance in a timely fashion (or allow you to pay for the repairs and deduct the amount from your rent).

> ➤ Your landlord cannot change your locks or have the utilities shut off or evict you without proper notification. To evict you, your landlord must get a court order.

> ➤ You have the right to break your lease if your landlord breaks important aspects of your lease relating to safety, health or necessary repairs.

> ➤ Landlords cannot seize your property unless you abandon your property (as defined by law). Failure to pay your rent is not abandonment. There are other legal actions that will be taken against you first (such as an eviction).

> ➤ Your landlord must give you an itemized report of any deductions from your security deposits (if any). Normal wear and tear cannot be deducted. The damage from the 300 holes in the wall where your dartboard used to be will be deducted from your security deposit.

> ➤ Most states require your deposit be refunded within a reasonable time period (usually 30-45 days after the end of your lease).

Hopefully you will never have to deal with any of these issues. In the unfortunate event your landlord does violate one (or more) of your rights, what do you do? You cannot just move out the next day. If you just leave and take your stuff with you, not only will you not get your security deposit back, but the landlord may actually be able to take legal action against you. On the other hand, it can be prohibitively expensive to take your landlord directly to court. What is the best way to resolve the issue?

The first thing you should do is speak with your landlord directly. Explain your concerns. It's possible the two of you can work everything out. If you come to some sort of agreement, either get it in writing, or write a letter yourself that details your agreement and send a copy to your landlord. This may help you to avoid any future misunderstandings. If that does not work you should try to contact one of the organizations that specialize in such disputes. You may be able to find an organization that will help you for free. Check out Appendix C and see if any of the information can help.

Perhaps you feel uncomfortable with your landlord and you want to move out. It is possible you can still work out an agreement to get out of the lease almost immediately, depending on what the issue is. Some landlords will let you break your lease for a fee. If you have serious issues (such as finding your landlord in your bedroom when you return from work), you should immediately contact one of the organizations listed in Appendix C.

Tricks To Save Money

There are no magical formulas or anything that will be able to help you save tons of cash. There are, however, several things you can do to minimize your apartment costs. Even if you are unable to negotiate a lower monthly rent you can try to save money in other ways relating to your apartment. Sometimes you have to be a little creative; other times you should just use common sense.

The first step is to thoroughly look around for a great deal on an apartment. Many of the large apartment complexes offer sign-on incentives such as free rent the first month or reduced rent for the first three months. Weigh the total cost with that of other apartments. In other words, if you can get an apartment for $600 per month, but another place offers one month free with the regular price of $800, you will still spend more for the $800 apartment in your first year ($800 x 11 months = $8,800 compared to $600 x 12 months = $7,200). See there, I just saved you $1,600. Too bad I don't work on commission.

As mentioned earlier, you should find out if your employer offers any type of moving service, relocation reimbursement, or even apartment recommendations. Perhaps you could ask your human resource contact to talk to some of the employees and see what they can tell you. If you know anyone in the area (assuming you are moving to a new area) see if you can stay with them for a few days before your job starts and use that opportunity to visit several apartments. Also, ask them if they know anyone who rents and find out what they recommend.

Once you have found at least one place you like, find out if there is any type of incentive. If they are not willing to offer an incentive, find out if any part of the contract is negotiable. Maybe the landlord would be willing to reduce the monthly fee slightly or even pay for some of the utilities. If nothing else, see if they will settle for a lower deposit (such as $250 instead of $500). The less money going out, the more you get to keep. Believe me, if you are moving, you need to hang onto every dollar you can. By the time you buy all of the little items (garbage cans, toilet scrubbers, shower curtains) you will have exhausted every last dollar of savings.

If you still haven't been able to save much money, or even if you have, there is more you can do. If you have an independent landlord (your building is owned by an individual and not a corporation), you may be able to save money by improving the apartment. Talk to your landlord and see if he or she would be willing to reduce rent one month if you paint the outside of the apartment house, or landscape the yard or even mow the lawn. Depending on your situation, and your skills, you may be able to save a few dollars here and there by doing a little handy work. If you don't know how to do any handy work yourself, call your dad. He's not sending you money anymore, so you might as well get something out of him, right?

Another way to save money is by reducing your utility costs. One quick way to reduce costs is to replace any air filters in the furnace (if they are really dirty). The furnace will not have to work as hard to push air through and your energy bill will be reduced. You can also replace the existing thermostat with a programmable one, unless your lease specifically disallows for any minor changes. You may want to get someone who understands wiring to do this for you. It is simple enough that even I was able to replace the one at my house without any problems and my home improvement skills haven't really moved past a hammer, a screwdriver and a lot of yelling to fix things around the house.

The programmable thermostat can be set to automatically reduce the heat at bedtime and while you are not home (during the winter) or reduce the air-conditioning during these same times (during the summer). Doing so saves in electricity costs by only using your furnace or air-conditioner when you actually need it. You could also just keep the standard thermostat and remember to set it back before you go to bed, but you won't have a nice comfortable home after work.

If you have any rooms in your apartment that you do not use, close the door to these rooms, and shut off any air vents. There is no use heating or cooling any rooms you do not use. You can buy magnetic covers that go over your closed vents to prevent any air from seeping through.

Chapter 7 Action Step

If you are getting ready to move into an apartment, check out at least one website and one local site or newspaper to research the average costs of an apartment.

If you are already in an apartment, then you get to pass on this chapter's action step. No strings attached!

Chapter 7 Summary

❑ Most apartments require a security deposit.

❑ Your landlord may check your credit history and ask for references from previous landlords... even the ones from college.

❑ You have certain rights as a tenant. Know them in case you need them.

❑ Look for ways to save money.

8
I Work, Therefore I Drive

There are several ways to get from one place to another. In college you probably walked, took a bus, or bummed a ride from someone who had a car. Perhaps you even used a bike or roller blades. While you can use those same methods to get to work, you will probably go with something more sophisticated such as a motorized scooter or a Segway. You might just choose the more traditional route and use public transportation or drive a car. No matter what method you choose to get to work, you will probably own a car at some point in your life. For instance, I used public transportation to get to work, but I used my car to get to the train station. I still used the car to go to the grocery store and the movies. In this chapter, we'll assume you are going to be purchasing a car sometime.

Here we go again. Another one of life's little ironies. In order to get to your job, you need a car. In order to buy a car, you need a job. Who came up with this system anyway? Sometimes it feels like the whole world has something against those of us who are just starting out. But wait… Just when it seems to get grim, you see that sign at the dealership, "No Credit? No Problem." Perhaps you've received one of those "checks" in the mail. If you haven't yet, you will. It looks like a check, from a car dealership or a major automaker in the amount of, say, $20,000. It is just a marketing gimmick to get you into the dealership.

So what is the deal with all of those auto dealerships that say credit is not an issue? Be very careful. What they will do is charge you an extra high interest rate on your loan and sometime additional fees, since you have a bad or no credit history. If you are worried about not having enough money for a down payment, you may still be able to go through a bank. Perhaps your parents will cosign. (Warning: I am not endorsing cosigning because way too often a person bites off more than they can chew, or they lose their job, or some other life event takes place and their parents get stuck with the bill). I know you want to be independent, but we all could use a little help. You may be able to refinance later and take their name off of the loan. Of course, if you follow our debt elimination plan, you'll have it paid off in just a couple of years anyway. Talk about making your parents proud. Maybe they'll even reimburse you for this book!

Okay, so what about that check in the mail? Actually, it is nothing more than a loan you *may* be qualified for in order to purchase a new car. It is somewhat deceptive. If you assume nothing in life is free, you should be able to avoid any of these "tricksters."

Prepare for the Sales Person Before You Walk onto the Lot

Once again, I am asking you to do a little homework. This time you may have a little more fun. You only need to do this one if you are thinking of buying a car. You can begin your search by going on the web. Visit *www.edmunds.com* or *www.kbb.com* (Kelley Blue Book). From these web sites you can find out exactly how much the dealer paid for the car (if it is new), or an estimate of what the dealer paid for the car if it is used. You can also determine how much your old car is worth if you are trading it in for a newer one. From there you can figure a good starting point in your negotiation process.

Salespeople make their living by selling things. I have nothing against honest salespeople, but I always keep in mind that it is in *their* best interest for me to buy from them even when it is not in *my* best interest. Sometimes the dealer may try to guilt you into purchasing a car after spending time with you or talking about some promotion they are very close to getting. This is not a charity function here. You have come to buy a car; the one that is right for you. Don't buy anything you do not want.

Another common tactic is where the dealer says they are giving you "the best possible deal." Then they "talk to their manager." After 15 or 20 minutes your salesperson returns and says the manager has allowed another few hundred dollars off, but that is as low as they can go, and that is already eating into your salesperson's commission. In reality, they were probably talking about golf or something for a few minutes. Either way it doesn't matter, because you should already know how much you are willing to spend.

You will quickly realize the whole process takes a very long time. I don't know the exact science here, but essentially you are being worn down ever so slowly. For one thing, you will have spent so much time at the dealership you might as well make the purchase because you cannot imagine going through this whole process again. Besides, most of your day is gone and who has the time to keep looking for cars when there is so much more you could be doing with your life?

If you do decide to make your purchase, make sure there is a clear understanding of what car you are getting, what features and warranties come with it and at what price. Before you go to the final "signature" room, tell the dealer ahead of time you want to be made aware of any possible extras such as extended warranties and so on because you will not add anything else to the sale when you go to sign the paperwork. Dealers make so much extra profit from those last minute sales. It goes something like this, "By the way, I forgot to mention that we also offer a rust proofing package. We could go ahead and add that on for only $10 per month. You'll hardly notice it in your payment. What's $10 a month to protect a $20,000 investment?" First of all, it is not an investment, it's a purchase, but that's another issue. Second of all, actually there is only a first. Like I said, you are already worn down at this point and you are more likely to agree to anything.

That's why you must ask before you sit down for the final signatures. Another way dealers try to take advantage of you is to ask, "Okay, everything looks good. You would like to protect your vehicle with our three year extended warranty wouldn't you?" Again, you want to know about all of this upfront.

Just for fun, here are a few other sales tactics to watch for. The salesperson will use the word "authorize" instead of "signature". "If you would just authorize this right here..." Everyone knows that when you sign something you are making an agreement and you should read everything first. Also, everything is referred to as an "investment" instead of a "purchase". "To protect your investment, you should..." Anything that is expected to decrease in value is not an investment. This includes cars and refrigerators.

When you begin to do your paper work, not only do you have to wait for a while, the dealer will seem agitated if you start to take time and think before making a decision. If you are going to spend that much money, I say take all the time you need.

There are several ways to shop for a car. You can take the traditional route, which is to browse a few dealerships until you find something that is almost what you are looking for and is close to the price you are willing to spend. Not only will you spend a lot of time, but you may also find yourself negotiating for a car on the lot before you are really ready. That means you will be negotiating about cars you know little or nothing about.

Perhaps the best way is to first shop online. That way you can see what types of cars are available and at what prices. You can also see what others have to say about various cars so you know which ones seem reliable and which ones have the most problems. After you do all of your online research you will be better equipped to find what you want and start negotiating prices.

Once you know exactly what you want, you can fax or email several different car lots within your driving range, and have them send you a quote. You should specify make, model and year, and what condition you want the car in (if it is used). Also, list any features the car must have such as air-conditioning and power door locks. You may also want to list anything you do not want such as any shade of brown or pink. Inform the dealerships you are interested in purchasing a car, based on the descriptions in your email or fax, and that you are sending your request to several dealerships to find out who has the best offer. Once you receive quotes, you can go to the dealership and test-drive the vehicles. If you find that the car is not really what you are looking for, then walk away. The salesperson will probably try to make you feel bad, but we are talking about *your* money here!

Thanks to our creative society there are several other options available for buying a car. Costco and Sam's Club offer car-buying services they claim will save you money. You can go directly to some of the auto manufacturer websites such as GM and Ford and build the exact car you want. From there you can enter your zip code and the dealerships in your area will send a quote to you within a couple of days. Some dealerships are now offering no-haggle pricing where they mark the car with the lowest price they are willing to accept, and you can either pay it or leave it. You can even go to e-bay and bid online for a car!

The one key ingredient, no matter which way you choose to shop for a car, is to know what you want. You should create a list of all the features you absolutely must have, the ones you would really like to have, and the ones you absolutely do not want. You also want to figure out how much you can afford. Remember, you may be paying for this car for a long time. If you start to think, "I can sacrifice a little more to get a slightly more expensive car," you may be slipping right into the dealer's hands. It is one thing to give up a few nights out one month for a car, but to do that month after month for five years will make you miserable.

Don't fall for the, "Well, you're young and you'll be getting raises so you'll make more money soon and the payment won't be that bad." Remember; when you take out a loan for a car (or anything for that matter) you are already giving up future income in order to enjoy your purchase today (see Chapter 10 for more information on debt). Don't start thinking about giving up future pay raises also! If you cannot comfortably afford the payment today (take into account other things you want to do with your money and the maintenance costs on the car), you simply cannot afford the payment. Stick with this advice and read Chapter 10 about getting out of debt and you could find yourself wealthier than you imagined in less than ten years.

Financing Your New Wheels

Now, let's discuss some of your financing options. Clearly, paying cash is the way to go. If you have enough money sitting around to buy your car without taking out a loan, this is the best method. Not only can you be free and clear of any ongoing monthly payments, but you can also negotiate a better deal. After all, the sale will be much easier to the dealer or the individual selling the car if you can walk up to them with a certain amount of money in a certified banker's check. They don't have to wait for financing approval and there is less paper work. You'll also notice that some car companies advertise the choice between low financing rates and cash back (for instance, 0% financing for 60 months or $3,000 cash back). Essentially, you are saving $3,000 in this example just for already having the cash available.

Assuming you are like most people, you don't have enough money lying around to buy a car. That means you are going to have to borrow money or lease. Have you decided which to do? The answer depends on how long you will keep your car. Basically, if you are the type to trade in your car for a newer model every three years, perhaps leasing is the way to go. Of course, if you plan to lease, maybe you should go back through this book and read a little closer. Otherwise, it makes more sense to buy your next car. By leasing a new car every three years, you never really own anything. You are simply renting the car for three years, and then renting a new one for three years, etc. You will constantly be paying for a car. You will never get to enjoy that brief period of time after you own the car outright, just before it dies.

Your best option, in this case, is to buy the car. Car loans are simple loans. You borrow a certain amount and pay a fixed payment every month, based on the interest rate and the length of the loan (three years, four years, five years, etc.). After the length of the loan (i.e. five years) your loan balance will be paid off and you are finally the proud owner of a car. Of course the warranty is usually over at this point, so be prepared to spend money for repairs.

There are three factors to your car loan that affect your payment; the amount borrowed, the interest rate and the length of the loan. The higher the interest rate, the higher your payment. The more you borrow, the higher your payment. The longer your loan, the lower your payment. Wow, it almost sounds like a low interest, low cost loan for as long as possible is the best deal, but it's not. You definitely want to get the best price you can for the car and get a loan for the least amount of interest, but you do not want to stretch your car payment for longer than you have to.

Sure, a six-year loan has a smaller monthly payment than a three-year loan, but you will be paying much more for your car. Here is an example. Assume you bought a $10,000 car with nothing down, so your total loan is $10,000. If the bank offers you two loans, both at 8%, but one loan is for three years and the other is for six years. The 6-year loan will have payments of $175 per month, but you will pay $2,623 in interest. The 3-year loan will have payments of $313 per month, but you will only pay $1,281 in interest. The 6-year loan may have smaller payments, but the car will cost you $1,342 more (you will pay double the interest to borrow the money).

Another problem with long-term car loans is that you will be upside-down on your loan. Upside-down means you owe more on your car than it is worth. How does this happen? In Chapter 10, on debt and credit, we will discuss that with most loans, you are paying much more money towards interest in the beginning and very little towards the principal. In the example above, if you would have chosen the 6-year loan, after three full years you would have still owed $5,600. The problem is that your car is probably only worth about 80% of that, or $4,800 since your car depreciates so quickly.

What's wrong with being upside-down? To begin, it is never a good thing to own something that takes away from your net worth. On top of that, what happens if you want to get rid of your car for some reason (too small, new child, new job, etc.)? If you sell your car, you will have to come up with the difference in order to pay off the loan.

Otherwise the bank, which holds a lien on your car, will not allow you to transfer the title. If you trade the car in to buy another one, you will have to apply the remaining loan balance towards your new car. In other words, if you still owe $7,000 and you trade the car in for $5,000, the remaining $2,000 will be added to the loan of your new car. For instance, if you purchase a new $18,000 car, your loan will be for $20,000. Now you will start out by being upside-down on your next car!

You can see how this leads to a vicious cycle that never gets any better. Another problem with being upside-down on a car is if you total it. If you are in an accident that badly damages your car, and your insurance company figures it is cheaper to pay you what the car is worth than to fix it (see Chapter 13), you may receive less than what you owe. Now you are stuck paying off a car you no longer even own. That's about as bad as it gets.

I know it is difficult to maintain the balance between getting a reliable car, making your monthly payment, and paying off your car as soon as possible. Nobody said it was going to be easy. Try to get a loan that will allow you to pay off the car within three years, while still having a little left over to pay for the maintenance costs. If you are able to do this with your first car, great, but I don't expect this out of most people until their next one. The longer your loan, the more you will pay. Is that $15,000 car really worth $18,000? You have to be the one to decide. If you find yourself wavering between two cars of different prices, or thinking about extending your loan, please read Chapter 10; maybe that will help sway you in the right direction.

Maintain Your Car to Keep it Problem Free

Perhaps one of the easiest ways to save money on your car is to maintain the one you own, or maintain the one you buy. I am the first to admit that I occasionally forget to change the oil, sometimes for months. When you are already being pulled in multiple directions at once, with your finances and your time, the last thing you want to think about is spending money on your car. We tend to only spend money on our car when it is having problems, instead of spending money to prevent it from having problems. As you go through this book you will start to look at things such as retirement, vacations, emergency funds, and paying off your debt. Once you get excited about doing all of these things with your money, little setbacks such as $80 for a battery and $300 for an alternator can really be frustrating. When we discuss cash flow issues, we'll try to help you build these little expenses into your budget. In the mean time, let's find some ways to keep your car running for as long as possible.

To find the specific maintenance recommendations for your car, you should consult the owner's manual. Generally, there are a few procedures that are standard for almost every vehicle.

Change your oil every three months or every 3,000 miles, whichever comes first

Don't think just because you drive short trips you can wait longer to change your oil. Driving short distances is actually harder on your car than long trips. Your engine does not have enough time to heat up. It's a little more technical than that, but I don't really understand and you don't have to either. Just change your oil every three months no matter how many miles you put on it. If you put a lot of miles on your car, change your oil every 3,000 miles even if it has only been a month since your last oil change.

Changing your oil does not have to be expensive. A quart of oil will cost between one and three dollars. An oil filter will cost another $5. So, for less than $10 you can change the oil yourself in about 20 minutes. If you are like me, and you fear the idea of tasting oil by accident, or have visions of leaving an oil trail in your driveway because you did something wrong, take your car to an oil lube shop. You can usually have the oil changed for about $20. Look for coupons. Most oil places will have coupons ranging from $3-$5 in the newspaper, on the back of grocery store receipts, and in those flyers you get in the mail.

Check your tire pressure monthly

Your owner's manual should tell you what tires to use and at what pressure they should be inflated. If you want, write that down in this book, or put it in your glove compartment, or on your calendar. Keeping your tires inflated properly will not only allow your tires to last longer, but will also keep your car more fuel-efficient. Having your tire pressure too low will reduce your car's gas mileage. Over-inflating your tires can be dangerous.

Rotate your tires every six months

Here is another way to keep your tires longer. By rotating them you will not be wearing any one tire significantly more than any other one. This could also help keep your car in alignment. If you live in a region where you have to use winter treads on your car for at least a few months every year, just have them rotated in the early spring and the late fall when you switch tires anyway.

Of course, almost every car has specific maintenance needs at various mileage levels. For instance there is usually a 10,000-mile, 30,000 mile and 60,000 mile maintenance recommendation. At these various levels you should be checking or replacing certain belts, hoses, etc. At specific times you will also need a tune-up or you may have to change your coolant. You should really consider these future costs when you are searching for your next car. You're not just looking at $250 per month for the payment. Your budget needs to be able to handle these maintenance costs as well. You can schedule them in with your list of goals. Follow the guidelines from Figure 8-1 and your car should last a long time.

In addition, for purposes of safety and convenience, here is a list of recommended items to keep in your vehicle. Obviously certain items are only needed in the winter.

- ❑ Jumper cables
- ❑ Spare tire & jack
- ❑ Flashlight & extra batteries
- ❑ Fire extinguisher
- ❑ First aid kit
- ❑ Duct tape
- ❑ Extra windshield washer fluid
- ❑ Heavy duty rags or paper towels
- ❑ Pair of work gloves
- ❑ Tie-down straps
- ❑ Ice scraper
- ❑ Blankets
- ❑ Mini shovel
- ❑ Small bag of sand for traction
- ❑ All-in-one tool kit (includes screwdrivers, hex keys, wrench, etc.)

As a general guideline, I have included a chart that will help you keep up with your car.

Every Month

- ❑ Check tires for inflation and wear
- ❑ Windshield washer fluid

Every 3 Months (Or 3,000 Miles)

- ❑ Engine oil (replace)
- ❑ Air filter
- ❑ Oil filter
- ❑ Fuel filter
- ❑ Power steering fluid

Every 6 Months (Or 6,000 Miles)

- ❑ Automatic transmission fluid
- ❑ Battery and cables
- ❑ Windshield wiper blades (replace)
- ❑ Lights (including blinkers)
- ❑ Hoses

Every 12 Months (Or 12,000 Miles)

- ❑ Brakes
- ❑ Cabin air filter
- ❑ Exhaust
- ❑ Chassis lubrication
- ❑ Coolant (antifreeze)

Figure 8-1: General Car Maintenance

Chapter 8 Action Step

Visit some of the car buying websites to get a better feel for what your next car will cost and what your current car is worth. Next, use the free calculators to determine what your monthly payment would be. Compare the total payments (and total cost) of a new car to a similar two-year old car and a similar three-year old car (and an even older one if you want).

Chapter 8 Summary

❑   Do your research before going onto the lot.

❑   Don't buy new if you can resist. You will get hit with most of the depreciation.

❑   Avoid leasing if at all possible. You pay for the most expensive part of the depreciation, with nothing to show for it in the end.

❑   The longer your loan, the more you will pay in interest. Try to pay off your car loan early. It is depressing to make payments on a car that is no longer under warranty.

❑   Proper maintenance will keep you safe and keep your car running longer. It will save you money in the long run.

9
Home Sweet Home
of Your Own

S o you really think you are ready to buy a home. What's that you say? You are not quite sure. Should you rent longer? Well, you have come to the right place. First we'll help you decide if you are ready to buy a home, then we'll decide if it makes sense financially. Finally, assuming it is your time to buy, we'll show you all you need to know about the home buying process from beginning to end.

One of the most common questions people ask is, "Should I rent or buy?" Purchasing a home is a huge commitment and is really a personal decision. If you are single and you really enjoy all of your free time, you are really busy taking graduate courses, or you are a young couple that really enjoys being on the go, home ownership may not be for you just yet.

Unlike taking care of a 600 square foot apartment, owning a home takes a lot of time and energy. Usually it takes longer to clean (since it is bigger than your apartment). Plus, you are also responsible for the outside (unless it is a condominium). I've heard more than one homeowner complain that they are *owned* by their homes instead of the other way around. Between the lawn care and the shrubs and the carpet, you will spend a few more hours cleaning. On top of that, you are also in charge of any repairs. If your roof gets a leak or your furnace quits working, there is no more calling the landlord. Now everything is your responsibility.

If that didn't scare you away, you have to ask yourself a few questions before you put in your first bid. How long are you going to stay in town? Are you going to be looking for a new job in the next six months? Will you want to move closer to work once you get your next raise? Will your financial situation change soon? What about marriage?

If you are going to be getting married in the next couple of years, you may want to make sure your partner also wants a home right away. As a rule, if you are going to be moving in the next three years, you should not buy a home. If you will be staying there for more than three years, homeownership may be a good idea, depending on the cost.

There are several exceptions to the rule. If you are relatively risky and you think the housing market is or will be tight and the prices will increase a lot, you may still want to buy a home and plan to profit from the resale. It is possible to do this, but highly unlikely in less than three years. Remember, sales commissions from real estate agents usually run about 8%. That means if you buy a home for $100,000, you have to resell it for almost $109,000 just to break even. There are other factors to consider also, such as how much money you put into the house while you were there, if the payments were more or less than what your rent would have been, how much you saved in taxes, etc. The key is that you would need a large jump in price in a short period of time to profit or even just to avoid losing money in the transaction.

Another exception (and this too is for risky investors) is if you will buy the house, live in it for a while, then move out and rent it to others. We will discuss real estate a little bit in the investing chapter. Suffice it to say rental property can be profitable, but it takes a lot of hard work; much harder than investing in the stock market.

Other factors to consider with owning a home include pride of ownership, the feeling of belonging to a community or owning a piece of the earth, or any other personal feelings that come into play. As mentioned earlier, buying a home is a very big commitment, but it is also a very personal one. Not every decision has to be based strictly on numbers.

With that said, if you have determined you are ready to buy a home, you should look to see if it makes financial sense. You can check your numbers on any one of several online calculators (see Appendix C) to see if it is cheaper or more expensive to own instead of rent.

Calculate Your Mortgage Costs

Once a person has determined they will buy a home, there are two fundamental financial questions that need to be answered. "How much can I afford?" and, "How much will the monthly payment be, based on the purchase price?" A mortgage broker or lender can most easily answer these questions. You could go to your local bank and ask to get "pre-qualified" for a mortgage. You should not pay anything to get pre-qualified. The lender will ask you a few basic questions such as your income, how long you have had your job, what your debt payments are and so forth. They will then be able to give you a rough estimate of how much mortgage you qualify for, and what your monthly payments will be.

Be sure to ask if they can give you an estimate of your monthly payments including taxes, insurance, etc. Most online calculators only tell you what your monthly principal and interest payment will be. If your agent does not give you an estimate, call a local settlement company and ask about the averages in the local area. It is a good idea to find a settlement agent (or attorney) anyway, although your real estate broker may be able to recommend one for you. If you still can't figure out how much to add for these other costs, assume you should add about 20% to your monthly payment. In other words if your pre-qualification shows your principal and interest payments will be $1,000, assume your total monthly payments will be about $1,200 (20% of $1,000=$200).

It is also a good idea to use an online calculator or a spreadsheet to calculate your payment on your own so you can compare your numbers with what the bank tells you. Don't hesitate to ask them to explain any differences. This also applies to any type of loan such as a car loan, etc. You should always be prepared to have your own calculated numbers to compare with what the sales person tells you. Figure 9-1 will help you estimate your monthly payments (not including taxes and insurance).

Getting pre-qualified is the easiest way to estimate what you can afford. If you are really serious about buying a home then you need to get "pre-approved." Pre-approval is more complex than pre-qualification. Your mortgage broker will ask for last year's W-2 (The form your employer sends you at the end of the year so you can report your taxes). They will also want your last several pay stubs, several bank statements and so forth.

Once you are pre-approved, the bank is basically guaranteeing you will be able to get a loan for that amount, as long as the house is appraised to be worth what you are paying. This tells the seller they are taking very little risk with you as a buyer, because the bank has already said you can get the loan for that amount. If someone else makes an offer on the house, but is not pre-approved, the seller has to wait to see if that person will even be able to borrow the money. Since you have already been approved, you are at an advantage. In many cases pre-approval will cost you money (up to $500). However, if you buy the home and get the mortgage, that $500 will be applied towards your closing costs.

Approximate Monthly Payment for a $100,000 Mortgage
Based on the Length of the Loan and the Interest Rate
(Principal and Interest Only – Excludes Taxes and Insurance)

Interest Rate

Years	5.0%	5.5%	6.0%	6.5%	7.0%	7.5%	8.0%	8.5%	9.0%
10	$ 1,061	$ 1,085	$ 1,110	$ 1,135	$ 1,161	$ 1,187	$ 1,213	$ 1,240	$ 1,267
15	$ 791	$ 817	$ 844	$ 871	$ 899	$ 927	$ 956	$ 985	$ 1,014
20	$ 660	$ 688	$ 716	$ 746	$ 775	$ 806	$ 836	$ 868	$ 900
25	$ 585	$ 614	$ 644	$ 675	$ 707	$ 739	$ 772	$ 805	$ 839
30	$ 537	$ 568	$ 600	$ 632	$ 665	$ 699	$ 734	$ 769	$ 805

Figure 9-1: Monthly Payment Chart

Before you get too excited about your new home-to-be, make sure you have enough money. I know you just went through the exercise above, but all you learned is what the bank is *willing* to lend you. That does not mean you have enough money or you can *afford* that much. Perhaps you like to take several vacations each year, or maybe you were saving to buy a new car. The bank does not care about these things. They simply let you know the maximum amount of money you can borrow. That doesn't mean you should be borrowing the maximum amount.

You also have to look closely at the closing costs (we'll discuss this more in detail in a moment). Many people are surprised they need to have several thousand dollars available at closing. There are attorney's fees, inspection fees, courier fees, lending fees, etc. Usually you can expect closing costs to be about 3% - 5% of your total loan amount. If you are borrowing $100,000 then you will need at least $3,000 to $5,000 at closing, in addition to your down payment.

There are several types of mortgages, but I'll try to break them down into simple categories. You can get a fixed rate mortgage (the same interest rate for the entire length of the mortgage), an adjustable rate mortgage (the rate adjusts according to one of the major financial indices) or a hybrid loan, which combines a fixed rate period, such as the first five years, with an adjustable rate period, which will be the remaining years on your loan.

The advantage of a fixed mortgage is that you never have to worry about your interest rate going up. Your mortgage payments will remain relatively flat over the years (with the exception of the escrow, which may increase due to rising taxes and insurance). The disadvantage is that fixed rate mortgages usually have a higher interest rate than their adjustable or hybrid counterparts.

With an adjustable rate mortgage, you almost always get a better rate initially, but the rates can rise (or fall in theory) according to one of the major financial indices. If you are only going to be in your house for a short period of time or have reason to believe rates will fall, this may be a good option for you. Otherwise, be careful with these mortgages. Some people use the low initial rate to qualify for a more expensive house than they could otherwise afford, but end up in foreclosure when the rates rise faster than their income. If you choose an adjustable rate mortgage, check to see how often the rates can rise (monthly, every six months, etc.), how much they can adjust each period (such as each adjustment can be no more than ½%) and how far they can adjust in total (rates may start at 6%, but can rise to as high as 10% for instance).

A hybrid loan is well suited for most young adults for many reasons. First, the rates are usually lower than a fixed rate mortgage, although slightly higher than an adjustable in most cases. The hybrid usually starts with five, seven, or ten years of a fixed rate, before the adjustable portion kicks in. If you have ever heard of the 7-year itch, then you know most people either move or refinance their mortgage within their first seven years in a home. Thus, if you pay more to get a fixed rate loan, buy down the interest rate by paying points up front, and then refinance in seven years, you wasted a lot of money compared to the person who had a 7-year or 10-year hybrid. Of course, even the hybrid is risky because you don't know where the interest rates are going to be in seven years.

Within these categories, you also have loans for different periods, or years. You can usually get anywhere from a 15-year loan to a 30-year loan (in 5-year increments). Obviously your payments will be higher with the 15-year loan, but you can usually get a better interest rate. Also, your payments are less than double the 30-year loan, even though you pay it off in half the time!

If you refer back to Figure 9-1, you can compare the monthly payments (per $100,000 borrowed) for loans of different lengths of years. Keep in mind the main advantage of the shorter mortgages is that you will be done making house payments a lot sooner. That could mean a whole lot of extra cash to play with at the end of each month. The interest rates are usually lower for a 15-year mortgage than a 30-year mortgage because the bank knows they are taking less of a risk with you by lending money for 15 years instead of 30.

Taking all of the information into account, you should be able to decide about how much of your hard-earned money you are willing to spend each month on a mortgage, how much you will have available at closing, and how long of a mortgage you are willing to suffer through. With a little research on the web, and at your local banks and mortgage companies, you should be well prepared for the financial piece of the home-buying process.

Beyond the Mortgage

Now that you have your finances squared away, it's time to find a real estate agent. Do you really have to use one? Yes and No. If you already know the house you want, especially if it is for sale by the owner, you can probably get away without using a real estate agent. You will just need a good attorney to write your contract. Otherwise I would use a real estate agent, at least for the first two or three homes you buy. One thing you need to know about real estate agents is that most of them work for the seller. Unless you specifically find a buyer's agent, which are becoming more popular, the agent is actually working for the seller.

Now you have to ask yourself, "What is it that I want out of my new home?" Unless you plan to stay in your home for the rest of your life, you have to consider what features would make the house easy to re-sell. Even if you do plan to stay in the house forever, you have to consider that you are not your parents' generation. You are much more mobile. Remember the seven-year itch? There is a very good possibility you will move within seven years of purchasing your first home.

You may not care which school district the home is in if you don't have any kids, but if it is a four bedroom home, then when you are ready to sell, families are more likely to look at it. And one thing most families consider is the type of schools in the area. You should also consider your commute to work and the distance to the nearest large city and any other amenities such as doctors' offices, grocery stores, etc. Not only should you consider such issues for your own liking, but also for potential buyers once you move out and sell. There are many more features you should consider about the home, the neighborhood, and the community you are considering.

Once you have an idea of the type of home you want and how much you are willing to spend, it is time to find a real estate agent. The best way to find a good real estate agent is to ask friends, family, neighbors or co-workers who have purchased a home if they would recommend their agent. While you are at it, ask them if they have any advice for you since they obviously went through this process at least once before. You may also be looking to purchase a new home from a planned community. They don't advertise this, but you can still use your own agent when buying from the builder in a planned community. If you don't, the sales person at the community usually makes more money. Remember, they work for the builder, not you.

Your agent will usually ask you some of the standard questions, such as "What is your price range?"; "What areas of the city or county are you are looking at?"; "How many bedrooms do you want?"; etc. It is not uncommon that the house you end up purchasing at the end of this long journey is completely different than the one you imagined when you began. It could be because the home prices were a lot different than you expected, or it could just be that once you saw what you described to the real estate agent it really wasn't what you expected.

Most experienced real estate agents are able to listen to what you say, and then find exactly what you mean. If your agent continues to show you the wrong homes after trying to give them feedback (such as ones way out of your price range or completely the wrong style), feel free to find a different agent. You are about to work with somebody to spend more money than you ever have before, so you want to make sure you can trust the person and they understand you.

Once you search online for different homes and visit several more with your real estate agent, you may finally find one or two that really work for you. Sometimes you are lucky just to find that one right home. Other times you may realize your expectations were too high and you need to find a "starter home" that better fits your budget. Either way, the process is just getting ready to heat up.

Your next step after you find the home you really want is to make an offer, which sounds easy enough… but just wait. First, you have to work with your agent to determine what a fair offer is for your home. Perhaps they are listed at 10% higher than previous similar home sales in the area. You may decide to offer them 90% of their asking price. A home's value is subjective after all. On the other hand, maybe their home is under-priced, or you feel you will die if you don't get that house. Then you may want to just offer them 100% of their asking price.

If the market is really tight, it may make sense to offer them a little more than they asked. You can even use an escalation clause. An escalation clause let's you make an offer of $100,000 for example, plus $1,000 higher than the highest offer up to $110,000. That means if somebody else offers $105,000 then your offer automatically becomes $106,000. Of course, once you show your hand, the seller can counter offer and ask for the full $110,000 since they know you are willing to go that high anyway. Just don't give away any more than you have to. You must be smart in your negotiations and try not to get too emotionally involved.

Speaking of emotions, I must say that buying a home is an incredibly emotional roller coaster. First, you have to absolutely fall in love with the home in order to be willing to spend that much money on it to begin with. To justify the cost (especially if you go above your original budget) you convince yourself of all of the positives (the master bedroom has a huge walk-in closet and the basement has a built-in game room) and ignore the negatives (we're not that close to work). So now you have decided that you love it so much you are willing to sign away hundreds or thousands of dollars every month for the next 30 years to get it. Then you make the offer and … wait.

You may wait for a few days before you hear anything from the seller. So after a few nights without sleep, you finally hear from your agent. Either the seller accepted your offer, rejected your offer, or made a counter-offer. If they accepted the offer, congratulations! But we'll get back to you. If they rejected your offer, then I am sorry for your disappointment, but that must not have been the right house for you. You've made it this long without your own home, so a little while longer, until you find the perfect home, won't hurt too badly. Hopefully your next experience will work out a little better. If you receive a counter-offer, be prepared for more roller-coaster emotions.

A counter-offer means they did not reject your offer, and they did not go with another buyer right away, but they want something more out of you. Perhaps they want more time before they have to move out, or they want some more money. This is where you have to decide what is most important to you. If the counter-offer is reasonable, you should probably take it. You don't want to regret losing the house because you refused to pay another $1,000 and move in a month later (unless your circumstances absolutely will not allow it). You can accept their counter-offer or counter back. Either way, you have to wait some more. Then, if finally accepted, you have a few contracts to sign, which your agent may deliver to you. At this point the settlement date is selected and you know when you will become the proud owner of a new home.

Then you go to settlement. This will be the time in your life where you sign more papers on one day than you have previously in your entire life combined. Although the settlement agent will probably try to rush you through the process, take your time and read the documents and look at the numbers. Remember, at this point you should already know how much you are paying for the house, how much your monthly payments will be and whether or not you have any extra payments such as PMI or a second mortgage. You are about to sign away a whole lot of money so do not let anyone rush you through this process.

When it is all over, you are finally the proud owner of a new home! Congratulations and enjoy your new home. Try to relax and celebrate before your first mortgage payment comes due.

Chapter 9 Action Step

Take a look at some home prices in your area (or whatever area you want to move to). Use some of the available online mortgage calculators to determine how much your monthly payment would be and what the total cost of the home would be with a 30-year and a 15-year mortgage.

Chapter 9 Summary

- Buying a home takes a lot of commitment and should be based on personal factors as well as the numbers.

- Calculate your mortgage costs before talking to your bank or mortgage lender. Remember, you also need to add taxes and insurance (approximately 20% extra) to your payment.

- Mortgage lenders will tell you the maximum they are willing to lend you, but that doesn't mean you can afford that much if you want to be able to do other things with your money.

- Prepare yourself for all of the time and effort involved in the home-buying process.

Part IV: Money Sense

"Money is not a goal; money is a tool to reach your goals"

10. Defeating Debt: Beat Lenders At Their Own Game

➤ Pay off your car loans and credit card debts

➤ Learn to live completely debt free by age thirty

11. How to Love 'em and Leave 'em… Your Student Loans, That Is

➤ Pay off your pesky student loans

➤ Know your options for repayment

➤ What happens if you don't pay them back

12. Save, Invest, and Save Some More

➤ Discover the 80-10-10 rule

➤ Make your money work for you, not the other way around

➤ Tackle the 401(k), IRA and other retirement decisions

13. A Financial Peripheral: Insurance

➤ Understand the basics of insurance coverage

➤ Get the right kind of coverage for life, health, disability and more

➤ Avoid the wrong kinds of insurance

14. A Life Less Taxing

➤ Understand your taxes to make them less scary

➤ Learn to fill out the basic tax form

➤ Explore your filing options, including electronic filing and paid preparers

10
Defeating Debt: Beat Lenders At Their Own Game

Before we get into the details of any particular type of loan, let's go straight to the bottom line. Debt is bad. Some people will argue with me on this point, but for someone in your age group, you should consider all debt to be bad debt. We'll talk about paying off your debt in a minute, but first let's talk about not getting into debt (or not getting into any more debt). Why is debt bad? Because you are spending tomorrow's income today. That means you might get that new toy today, but if you have to go to work tomorrow to pay for something you already enjoyed, where is the fun in that? Imagine that you eat at a nice restaurant on Friday night. By Monday the whole memory of the meal has faded, yet there you are at work earning money to pay for last Friday's meal. That means you get nothing out of working that day, because you already enjoyed it in the past.

Now let's say you buy a new computer for $1,000 on your credit card. You pay the minimum $20 every month. After three years the computer is outdated. You still owe about $790 on your credit card. So if you decide to pay off your credit card, the next $790 that you earn will be paying for a computer you no longer have. In other words, to buy a new computer, you first have to earn $790 to pay off your debt, and then earn another $1,000 after that before you can buy a new one.

For the record, the $1,000 computer you bought the first time cost you a total of $1,400 if you include the interest charges on your credit card. If you stretch it out by paying only the minimum amount on your card, it will take more than 15 years to pay it off and you will have paid $1,300 in interest, for a total cost of $2,300. I hope it was a really good computer.

By getting yourself into debt, not only do you sacrifice your future income, but you also are paying more for everything once you include the interest charges. You are selling away your choices. If you have $1,000 cash you have many choices of what to do with that money. Once you spend it you have fewer choices, but at least you can go earn more. However, if you borrow another $1,000, you have even fewer choices, because now some of your future money has been spoken for. For instance, you cannot quit your job since you first have to earn that $1,000 you borrowed. If you lose your job, you are forced to get another one immediately, even if it is not the one you want, since you have to make the payments on your debt.

In addition, you are not saving anything because you are too busy making payments. What could be worse than spending the next three years waking up at five o'clock in the morning, commuting for 30+ minutes, staying late at the office, etc. only to look back and realize all you have to show for it is a computer that no longer works and about $790 in debt? Avoiding debt (this includes avoiding new debt if you already have some) is the first step towards reaching any financial goal. Paying off your current debt is the second.

Pay off Your Car Loans and Credit Card Debts

Most people will have some type of debt to contend with at some point in their lives. Some have car loans, others have credit cards, and some have a little bit of everything. No matter how big of a hole you dig yourself into, it is almost always possible to work your way back out in a relatively short time period.

What do I mean by relatively short time period? Well, that depends on how you look at it. If you have $2,000 worth of credit card debt and no loans, you should be done in a matter of months. If you are starting out with $40,000 in student loans and $5,000 in credit card debt, we may be talking about four or five years. Sure that may seem like a long time, but look at your numbers again. Paying off $45,000 in less than six years is quite incredible for someone just starting out.

Conventional wisdom says you should begin by paying off your highest interest rate debt first. I am by no means conventional. In my experience with people, immediate gratification goes a long way. In other words, I recommend paying off the debt that can be paid off the fastest. In some cases this will be the smallest debt, in other cases it will not. Here is how you figure out which debt to pay off first.

List all of your debts. Write down your monthly payment beside each of your debts. Now, divide the debt by the monthly payment (that should be the big number divided by the small number). Write down the answers beside each debt (See Figure 10-1). The smallest answer is the one that will be paid off first (If you prefer to skip the math calculation then just list your debts in order of smallest to largest. It will be close enough). You should focus all of your resources onto this debt. What I mean is that any extra money you pay towards your debt should be directed towards this one. Pay only the minimum on the rest of your debts.

Once the first debt is paid off, take the amount you had been paying each month and add that to the next debt on the list and so on. By the time you get to the last debt, you will be paying the same amount per month as you always had, but it will all be going towards one debt. Using this strategy will knock years off the life of your debt. Look at Figure 10-2 to see an example.

Order of Debt Payoff

	Amount Owed	Payment	Calculation	Ranking
Student Loan	$ 25,000	$ 270	92.6	5
Car Loan	$ 12,000	$ 360	33.3	2
Personal Loan	$ 2,000	$ 65	30.8	1
Credit Card 1	$ 1,000	$ 25	40.0	3
Credit Card 2	$ 850	$ 18	47.2	4

Figure 10-1: Sample Order of Debt Payoff

To make things go even faster, we are going to look at ways to add to the minimum monthly payments. One of the reasons we discussed stretching your paycheck earlier was to find extra money each month to add towards your debt payments. That was a bit sneaky, wasn't it? Well that's how I operate. Don't worry; I'm not going to force you to sit in the dark with no television for the next four years eating nothing but rice and Ramen noodles (after all, that's what college was for). It only takes a little bit to go a long way. If you can add just a few dollars a month to your payments, you will be thanking yourself again and again a few short years from now.

Learn to Live Completely Debt Free by Age Thirty

Okay, for those of you who are already over thirty (or almost there) this is still relevant, but just tack on about five years or so from your current age. For those of you under the age of twenty-five, including you recent grads, you really can be debt free by age thirty. You start by plugging the leaks. Your first priority (after you get a job, place to stay and so on) is to manage your spending so you are spending no more than you earn.

If you are still single, controlling your spending may actually be more difficult than you first imagined. You will be tempted to continue living the college lifestyle... but with money. When you meet new people or hang out with old friends it will seem like no big deal to spend your money dining out, going places, or even paying for other people, since it seems like you are just making so much. Don't believe me? Spend about five hours out one Friday night with a group of friends and see if you can spend less than $50. Now, if you are paying for a date, you'll be lucky to get away with spending less than $100 on a weekend night. I have also observed that when one or two people among a group of friends earn more than the others, they tend to subsidize their income-challenged friends. I am not against spending money for your friends, but just make sure you are not going into debt to do it. If you can manage to financially break even your first year after college, I'm not going to complain.

Once you get a year of spending (without going into debt) under your belt, it is time to start thinking about your future. No, not your retirement in 40 years, I'm talking about your late twenties and early thirties. You know, when you will be getting married, taking a honeymoon, buying a home, purchasing a new car, and so on. Perhaps before I talk about how to get out of debt so quickly, I should explain why you would want to. It's about choices. Our society is all about choices. Do you want the small, grande, or super size? Would you like cream or sugar? Tomatoes? White or wheat? Would you like a sunroof? I think you see where I am going. We like choices. Debt takes choices away from us. Let's look at the following scenario:

You graduate from law school with $90,000 in student loans. You have just decided you no longer want to practice law, or you want to open a clinic to help the underprivileged. Guess what? You can't. You see, that $90,000 is now hanging over your head. Having such a large debt has limited your choices. You now *have* to take a job that pays a high salary, even if it is not doing what you want, because of your debt.

Here is another scenario:

You get a job that pays $60,000 per year (perhaps in an expensive area). You accumulate debt that costs about $700 per month ($300 car payment, $200 in student loans and $200 in credit card debt). You are bringing home over $3,000 per month, so even if rent is $1,000 per month you are doing okay. Now, let's assume something in your life changes. Maybe you want to join the Peace Corps, or go on a mission trip, or perhaps move to a small town or change careers. Guess what? You can't. You are now stuck because of all of that debt. Suddenly, your money controls you, instead of you controlling your money. You have just limited your choices by getting into debt.

Having debt eliminates many of your choices, or at least makes them more difficult to pursue. By paying off your debt early in life, you can open up so many new choices for yourself. In fact, one of the greatest advantages of not having any debt is that you can use more of your money to save towards a future goal, even if you do not yet know what that goal is. Perhaps when you are ready to get married you will be able to take a nice honeymoon or make a nice down payment on a house (a mortgage is still debt, but we will pay that off very quickly also). If nothing else, you could eventually have more money for your retirement, or perhaps you will even retire early. I know I enjoy looking for those cheap last minute travel fares (Nassau for $250 roundtrip or Belize for $299). If you do not have any debt, and you have been saving money each month, there is no telling what you could do with your life.

Using the strategy mentioned earlier in this chapter, you could really be debt free in less than five years. If you buy a home during that time, you could still be debt free by age thirty. Most people just assume they will always have a house payment and a car payment but that is just not true. Once you have paid off your home and your car (as well as all of your other debt) most of your paycheck will be "play money." Aside from taxes, utilities and a few other things, none of your dollars will already be accounted for.

Let's start looking at a few simple ways to be debt free in as little time as possible. We will assume that for at least one year after graduation you were either living large, or you simply did not make enough to get by. Since then you either found a less expensive place to live or you found a roommate (unless your rent is already a great deal). In this example you are now 23 years old. You have received a $2,000 raise at work and you can easily make all of the minimum payments on your debts.

In this example you have the following debt and monthly payments:

Credit Card	$3,000	$75
Student Loans	$15,000	$225
Car Loan	$12,000	$250
Rent	---	$650
Utilities	---	$150
Car insurance	---	$100
Totals	$30,000	$1,450

With an income of $30,000, you can expect to bring home about $800 per paycheck (every two weeks), after deducting for taxes, insurance, 401(k), etc. With your $2,000 raise, you are now bringing home an extra $55 per paycheck (or $110 per month). Since you already survived on $150 per month last year (that is what was left after you paid your bills), you can increase your spending by $70 per month and still have an extra $40 to use towards paying off your debt.

Your best bet is to increase your credit card payment to $115 per month. Over the next year you will pay down an extra $500 on your card. In addition, since you are paid every two weeks, you get two extra paychecks per year (during two months you get a third paycheck). If you use $500 from one to pay for a vacation and $500 from the other to pay for Christmas gifts, you will still have an extra $710 to put towards your credit card. At the end of the year, your credit card balance will be about $1,600. If you repeat this plan for another year, you will have your credit card paid off completely by age 25.

Now you can use the $155 (another pay raise where you added $40) per month you had been paying towards your credit card and use that towards your car. By the way, your car debt is now only about $7,375. By paying a total of $405 per month on your car, plus the additional $710 per year from your two extra paychecks, your car will be paid off completely, well before your 27th birthday.

Now you have an additional $405 to add towards your student loans, plus another $40 from your most recent pay raise. You are paying a total of $620 towards your student loans, plus an additional $710 per year from your extra paychecks. Since the balance is now only $10,900, you will have it paid off by your 28th birthday!

Let's quickly review our example. You got a $2,000 raise each year, and only used less than half of that additional money to pay off debt, so you still got to spend most of your raise. You used $355 from each of your two extra paychecks per year. Notice that you continued to use $355 even though your paychecks were getting bigger because of your raises. That means more money for Christmas and vacation. You are now 28 years old and you have no debt. Plus, you now have an extra $620 per month that no longer has to be used towards debt. What are you going to do with all of your money? I'm always accepting donations. Actually, you can treat yourself to a very nice vacation this year, or save it towards a house, or car, or do both!

If you are wondering, by the time you turn 30, assuming you save the $620 per month, you will have saved about $15,000. Even more exciting is being in a position where you don't owe anyone anything. Aside from your apartment lease obligation, you can go wherever you want. If you are not happy with your job, or you just want to move to the beach, there is nothing to stop you. Maybe you just want to enjoy the freedom for now. The choice is yours. Your money is no longer controlling you.

Okay, it seems like everybody has debt, so why is it so important to pay it off? To begin, not everyone has debt. Many wealthy people you see do not have any debt. In fact, many people were only able to acquire all of their wealth because they had no debt. You have already seen how debt takes away your choices. Most people who earn their way into millionaire status do so by saving heavily, spending lightly and avoiding debt as much as possible. Let's take a look at some numbers that illustrate how damaging debt can be.

Assume for a moment that you have $3,000 in credit card debt at 16% interest. Your monthly payment is probably about $60. If you pay just the $60 minimum payment, $45 goes towards interest and just $15 goes towards your principal. This means next month, assuming you do not add any other charges onto the card, your balance will be $2,985. If you continue to make only the minimum payment it will take you over 29 years to pay off the card! By the way, you will have paid $5,300 in interest on your $3,000 charge over that time period, and that is under the assumption you never made any new charges. Now are you ready for the real kicker? If you would have been saving those interest charges during that same time period and earned an average 8% return, you would have $30,000.

Let's recap. For the past 29 years you have paid over $5,300 in interest to a credit card company and you have exactly zero dollars to show for it. If you had invested the interest only portion of your payments for the last 29 years instead, you would have $30,000 in savings.

Age: 23		Age: 24	
Starting income	$32,000	Annual income	$34,000
Starting Debt Balance	35,000	Debt Balance	29,400
Bring-home monthly pay	1,710	Bring-home monthly pay	1,820
Monthly expenses	1,450	Monthly expenses	1,450
Extra monthly towards debt	40	Extra monthly towards debt	80
Extra towards debt from pay	710	Extra towards debt from pay	710
Spending money	220	Spending money	290
Age: 25		**Age: 26**	
Annual income	$36,000	Annual income	$38,000
Debt Balance	22,125	Debt Balance	14,515
Bring-home monthly pay	1,930	Bring-home monthly pay	2,040
Monthly expenses	1,450	Monthly expenses	1,450
Extra monthly towards debt	120	Extra monthly towards debt	160
Extra towards debt from pay	710	Extra towards debt from pay	710
Spending money	360	Spending money	430
Age: 27		**Age: 28**	
Annual income	$40,000	Annual income	$42,000
Debt Balance	6,905	Debt Balance	0
Bring-home monthly pay	2,147	Bring-home monthly pay	2,255
Monthly expenses	1,450	Monthly expenses	900
Extra monthly towards debt	200	Extra monthly towards debt	0
Extra towards debt from pay	710	Extra towards debt from pay	0
Spending money	500	Spending money	**1,355**

Figure 10-2: Sample Payoff Scenario

Here is another depressing example. Let's assume you have a car that runs well, but it is six years old and out of style, so you decide to trade it in. You buy a new car for $21,000 minus the $2,000 trade-in for your old car, so your loan is for $19,000 at 6% for five years. At the end of the five years your car will be worth about $4,000. Your total payments over the five years were $22,039. In the end, the car cost you $24,039 including interest. If you would have held onto your old car instead, and invested those payments at 8%, you would have $27,000 in savings.

In other words the $21,000 car actually cost you $23,000 in five years. Ouch. Of course, you may be thinking, "So I paid a little extra for the car, what is the big deal?" The big deal is that instead of having $27,000 in cash the next time you want to purchase a car, you will have to get another loan, and deal with another trade-in and the vicious cycle continues. Using the method I just showed you, with just five years of sacrifice (driving a car that may be 'out of style') you will never have to borrow money ever again to buy a car. Of course you will continue to set money aside every month for your next car, but instead of losing a portion due to interest payments on your loan, you are actually gaining a portion due to interest payments (or earnings) on your investment.

So why does the interest work so hard against you? I'm glad you asked. It's called compound interest, and when you are on the borrowing end of the deal (such as when you take out a loan or use a credit card) the compounding works against you. But, when you are saving and investing, that's when the power of compounding works for you. In Chapter 12 we are going to look at ways to save and invest, and how you can use compound interest to make your money work for you.

Chapter 10 Action Step

If you were following along earlier in this chapter, then you should already be done with this action step, but if not, now is your chance to catch up. List all of your debts. Write down your monthly payment beside each of your debts. Now, divide the debt by the monthly payment (that should be the big number divided by the small number). Write down the answers beside each debt. The smallest answer is the one that will be paid off first (See Figure 10-1).

Chapter 10 Summary

❑ Debt is when you spend money you have not yet earned; by spending money before you earn it, you will eventually have to give up future opportunities to pay for something that may have long expired.

❑ The more debt you have, the fewer choices you have to do what you want with your money.

❑ With just a little bit of discipline and patience, you can pay off your debt and remain debt free, which will open up a world of opportunities for you.

❑ To truly become wealthy, you need to stop owing so you can start saving.

11
How to Love 'em and Leave 'em... Your Student Loans, That Is

Y ou finally made it through all the tests, papers, and parties. Now that you are ready to begin life as a real adult, you also have to deal with those pesky college loans. It really does not seem fair. You went through all of those years of pain and suffering and now you have to pay for it!

Remember all those classes you took and the books you bought and maybe even the concerts you went to? Do you remember how you were able to afford those things while making very little money working? For so many students, student loans are what got you through all those years when you were broke in college. Whether you like it or not, once you graduate your student loans become a reality. As you begin to adjust to your new life after college, such as paying for everything yourself, you need to think about how you will repay your student loans.

Manage Your Student Loans Before They Manage You!

The great news is that there are a ton of options available to you for almost every situation. No job yet? There's a solution for you. Income way below what you expected? There's a solution for that as well. You want to pay off your loans as soon as possible or only make one payment every month for all your loans? Done. The point is federal student loans are the most borrower-friendly loan you will have in your entire life. They are designed to make sure you can always afford your payments no matter your situation. The key is to work with your lenders to make sure you manage your loans and payments according to where you are in your life and understand the consequences of borrowing. That way your loans do not end up managing your finances or take you in a direction you never wanted to go.

Know What You Owe

What type of loans do you have? Are all of your student loans federal student loans, private student loans or a mix of both? Are they Direct Loans, Federal Family Education Loans (FFELP), Perkins Loans or institutional loans? Why does this matter? Because the type of loan determines what you will pay, the interest rate, grace period, and how long you will have to repay. So before you graduate ask your financial aid office to provide a list of all of your student loans that have been processed through their office. If you have transferred from another college or university, you want to contact their financial aid office as well. Your goal is to collect as much information as you can about who you have borrowed money from to attend college.

Now that you have the information from the colleges you attended, it is time to consult the National Student Loan Data System (NSLDS) at *www.nslds.ed.gov.* The NSLDS is the U.S. Department of Education's central database for federal student loans. All of your federal student loans will be listed in this database, which includes the types of loans, the lender, the loan servicer, the loan amounts, the dates the loans were originated and disbursed, if the loans were cancelled, the outstanding principal and any outstanding interest due on the loans. Each individual loan is listed in the database as well as the total outstanding principal and interest for all loans. You can verify the disbursement amounts provided by your college financial aid office when compared to the NSLDS. Keep in mind that non-federal student loans will not be listed in the NSLDS, which is why you want to get a list of loans from your financial aid office.

Add up the total disbursements according to your financial aid office and make sure it matches what you find in the NSLDS. If it appears that you borrowed more than what the NSLDS indicates, then you probably have some private student loans as well. If it appears the other way around, then you should contact the Department of Education to verify your loan information.

Once you straighten out all of your loan amounts and who you owe, you should list these loans in a chart that shows who you owe, how much you owe, what your interest rates are, what your monthly payments are, when your payments are due, and the contact information of your loan servicer in case something goes wrong or you have questions. Keep this chart somewhere handy such as your laptop, smart phone, or in your top desk drawer at work if you prefer to keep track of it on paper.

If you are not confused yet then lucky you! Most students get lost somewhere between the lender and the loan servicer. Why are so many different people involved in the process? You just want your loan, your degree, and a job. A loan servicer is a company that is hired by the lender or by the Department of Education to manage the interaction between you and the lender. You will make your loan payments to a servicer. For most federal student loans you will deal with a servicer that is acting on your lender's behalf. It is important to know who your servicer is and how to contact them. The contact information is listed on NSLDS.

Choose Your Repayment Plan

Remember when I said federal student loans are borrower friendly? Here is proof – just one of many examples – you get to choose the repayment plan that fits best with your budget. You will be offered several repayment choices by your servicer, which we will discuss. If you do not choose any of the options available to you then you will automatically be placed in the standard payment option.

Standard Payments

A standard repayment plan on a federal student loan is designed to last 10 years. Your monthly payment will essentially remain the same (a fixed payment amount) and your loan will be paid off after 120 payments.

Graduated Payments

A graduated payment plan simply means that your payments start out smaller, but typically increase every few years and your payment may eventually be larger than what your standard monthly payment would have been. Your monthly payment will always cover at least the interest and will not be more than three times the amount of any other payment. So if your initial payment is $100 a month, none of the subsequent payments can be larger than $300. Typically your loan is repaid over 10 years.

Extended Payments

The extended repayment plan has a fixed monthly payment (it does not change) but your loan can last up to 25 years. You will have smaller monthly payments but they will last much longer and you will pay a lot more in interest. This plan is only available if you have more than $30,000 in federal student loans. Under this plan you may also be able to choose a graduated extended payment that increases every few years.

Payments Based on Income

There are also three payment plans that consider your income when determining your monthly payment amount.

Income-sensitive repayment (ISR) is an option for borrowers with FFELP loans. It is lender-driven and is not used nearly as often as other income-based plans. The payment is based on your annual income and the maximum repayment period is 10 years. You will have to ask your particular lender for the details and eligibility of this particular option.

Two other income-based plans are available that offer longer-term solutions. Income-contingent repayment (ICR) for borrowers with Direct loans, and income-based repayment (IBR) plans both consider your annual income, family size, and the state you reside in to determine the maximum you can afford to pay. One advantage of these plans is that the remaining portion of your loan may be forgiven (you won't owe any more on the loan) at the end of the repayment period. If the payment is less than the monthly payment for the standard ten-year repayment amount, and you cannot afford to make the payments any other way, then you may benefit from an income-based plan.

There are two things to consider if you are contemplating an income-based repayment plan.

First, it means your loan could end up lasting much longer than ten years. In fact, it could be stretched out to as long as 25 years, which means you pay interest over a longer period. The longer you make payments, the more you will end up paying in interest.

Second, if the payment ends up being less than the amount of interest you owe each month, the interest may still be due and it simply gets added to the amount you owe, which means you will owe even more money – maybe even more than you originally borrowed!

More information about the IBR plan is available in the "Repayment Plans" section at *www.studentaid.ed.gov* or visit *www.ibrinfo.org*.

Regardless of which plan you choose, if your monthly payment is based on your income, you are required to reapply annually and submit documentation to verify your income.

A word of warning about variable interest rate loans and repayment options: If you have a variable interest rate on your federal student loan, or interest is being added to your loan balance (which is called capitalization), your monthly payment amount may be adjusted accordingly. If your interest rate goes up or your loan balance goes up you can expect your monthly payment to go up as well. The payments get adjusted so your loan will still be paid off in the correct amount of time.

Comparing Your Repayment Options

What are the differences in monthly payments and total interest paid when comparing different repayment options? Look at Figure 11-1 for a comparison.

As you can tell by Figure 11-1, you want to choose the repayment option that is the most practical for you and not just the one that is most convenient. It may seem convenient to choose the extended payment since it is $160 per month less at just $243, but you will be in debt for 25 years and pay a total of $37,879 in interest! That means if you graduate at age 22 you will be just finishing up when you turn 47 years old! That is almost another whole lifetime.

Of course, if you simply cannot afford $403 monthly payments on the standard payment plan, then you may need to choose one of the other options for now. But keep in mind you can always pay extra on your loans as your income increases or switch back to the standard repayment plan if you do not think you will pay more than the minimum on your own.

Changing Your Payment Plan

With some exceptions, you can switch from one repayment plan to another at least once a year. For instance, if you asked for a graduated repayment plan because your budget was very tight, but you get a great new job that pays a lot more the following year and you decide you would like to pay off your loan sooner, you can switch to a standard repayment plan. On the other hand, if you decide to start out with a standard repayment plan then quickly realize you need lower payments for a few years, you can switch to the graduated plan and so forth. Contact your servicer about how and when you can change your repayment plan.

Figure 11-1: Sample Loan Repayment Option Comparison

Federal student loan repayment options assuming $35,000 owed upon repayment at 6.80% fixed interest rate.

	Monthly Payment	Interest Paid	Total Amount Paid	Years in Debt
Standard Repayment	$403	$13,333	$48,333	10
Extended Fixed Repayment	$243	$37,879	$72,879	25
Extended Graduated Payment	$198	$43,939	$78,939	25
Graduated Repayment	$277	$15,944	$50,944	10
Income-Based Repayment*	$172	$37,759	$72,759	21

Source: Student Aid on the Web, online calculators. Source for Income-Based Repayment: Finaid.org online calculator.

Prepaying Your Federal Student Loan

Prepaying a loan simply means paying it off early. There is no penalty for paying off a federal student loan early. In fact, depending on your circumstances, it usually makes good sense to do so. You can make extra payments or add extra money to your regular payments. Any extra money you pay towards your student loan will first go to pay off any accrued interest, and then the rest will be used to reduce your loan amount.

When you make an extra payment or add money to your regular payments you should specify that you want the money applied to the principal balance of your loan. Otherwise your servicer may apply the extra dollars towards your next payment. If you pay enough extra to cover a full monthly payment amount without indicating the money should go to principal, the servicer may assume you are making your next payment and may advance your payment due date. Since the purpose of the extra payments is to get out of debt sooner, that would defeat the purpose.

Loan Forgiveness Options

You may be eligible to have part or all of your student loans forgiven (your balanced gets wiped out so you owe no more) if you choose certain careers or meet other requirements. You can find out more about this option for federal loans at *www.studentaid.ed.gov* in the "Repaying Your Loans" section. Sometimes employers or federal or state governments will forgive your student loans or make your payments for you if you are willing to choose certain types of positions, such as a school teacher, primary care physician, or public service worker.

While student loan forgiveness may be a great benefit in some cases, it should only be one small part of your overall consideration for choosing a job and should not be your primary or only reason for doing so. There are many requirements that you will have to meet to take advantage of this option. Carefully consider whether you are willing and able to meet all these requirements to take advantage of the opportunity.

For example, let's say you have followed all the advice about getting a job and you have multiple offers. After careful consideration of all your options you have decided to choose the offer from the federal government and work as a public servant. To take advantage of the public service loan forgiveness benefit you have to make all of your payments over the next ten years. Any remaining balance on your student loans could be forgiven, which means that anything you still owe after ten years you will no longer have to pay.

How good is this benefit? For starters, this program requires you to work for a qualified public service employer while you make 120 monthly payments (10 years). That could limit your career choices during that time. Second, if you have a standard 10-year payment plan, your loan balance could be zero before you get a chance to take advantage of this loan forgiveness benefit. In other words, this benefit may help you if you choose to go into a public service job, but you should not base your career choice on this loan forgiveness option.

Consolidating Your Federal Student Loans

Consolidation simply means combining your loans into one. That means instead of having multiple loan payments to different servicers, you can consolidate your federal student loans so you have one payment. In addition, if your loans total more than $7,500 you may be able to reduce your monthly payments and stretch your loan repayment to more than 10 years, and possibly as long as 30 years. Of course, the longer it takes you to pay off the consolidated loan the more you will pay in interest over the life of the loan. Figure 11-2 indicates how long you can stretch your repayment according to the amount you owe.

If you have both subsidized and unsubsidized federal loans you can consolidate them so that you have one monthly payment. Your loan will simply have two parts to it in order to make sure your subsidized and unsubsidized amounts are still treated separately. That will matter to you if you end up going into deferment at some point, or if you return to college at least half-time. The subsidized portion of your consolidation loan will not accrue interest while the unsubsidized portion will.

Please note that consolidation loans do not have a grace period. That means if you consolidate your loans during the six-month grace period after you graduate or leave college your first payment begins 60 days after the consolidation takes place. If you want or need to take advantage of your six-month grace period then wait until the last month of your grace period before consolidating.

Total Federal Student Loans	Repayment Period May Not Exceed
Less than $7,500	10 years
$7,500 - $9,999	12 years
$10,000 - $19,999	15 years
$20,000 - $39,999	20 years
$40,000 - $59,999	25 years
$60,000 or more	30 years

http://loanconsolidation.ed.gov/examples/repyperiod.html

Figure 11-2: Consolidation Repayment Time Periods

Your federal student loans may have different interest rates. Some of your loans may have fixed interest rates while others may have variable interest rates (the rate can change). Consolidation loans have a fixed rate, so if you consolidate a variable rate loan you eliminate the risk of the interest rate going up. You also give up the potential for the interest rate to go down, but the security of a fixed rate is usually worth the trade-off, especially if your loan was issued during periods of low interest rates.

So how do you know what your interest rate will be if you consolidate? The government will use a weighted average formula which basically means there is no interest rate advantage or disadvantage to consolidation. A weighted average means the interest rate on the loan with the largest dollar amount will count a little more than the interest rate on the loan with the smallest dollar amount. In other words, if you have one loan at 6% for $10,000 and one loan at 4% for $5,000, your interest rate will not be a simple 5% (The average of 6% and 4% is 5%). Instead the larger loan with a 6% rate will count more. Since your total loan amount is $15,000 ($10,000 + $5,000 = $15,000), then the 6% loan represents 2/3, or 67%, of the total amount owed ($10,000 / $15,000 = 2/3 or 67%). The 4% loan only represents the remaining 1/3, or 33%, of the loan ($5,000 / $15,000 = 1/3 or 33%).

That means your new interest rate will be 5.33%, rounded up to the nearest 1/8%:

$$67\% \times 6\% = 4.00\%$$
$$+$$
$$33\% \times 4\% = \underline{1.33\%}$$
$$5.33\%, \text{ rounded up to } 5.375\%$$

Before you consolidate your loans make sure you carefully compare the advantages and disadvantages. You may lose benefits or rewards that were offered by the lender when you initially took out the loans. Only you can determine if the benefits of the new consolidated loan outweigh any benefits you may lose on your individual loans.

Consolidating Private Loans

Now you can graduate and consolidate all your student loans so you have just one single payment, right? Not so fast. You can only consolidate your *federal* student loans together. You cannot consolidate your private student loans with your federal student loans. If you have both private and federal student loans your private student loans will have to be repaid separately. The good news is that you may be able to consolidate all of your private student loans together as well. That means you could reduce all of your loans down to just two consolidation loans so you have only two payments.

While federal student loans have various protections, including no consolidation fees, you will have to look carefully at the fine print for any consolidation you do with your private loans. The private lender willing to consolidate all of your loans may calculate your interest rate any way they choose. There may be prepayment penalties.

Most private loans have a variable interest rate (which means the interest rate can change). While a variable interest rate may not be of much concern if interest rates are low, consider the consequences if the rate increases. If you have a $20,000 loan at 6% for 10 years your payment will be $222 per month. If the interest rate increases to just 8% your monthly payment increases to $243. If the rate increases as soon as you graduate, you will pay an additional $2,520 in interest over the life of the loan. A 10% rate would result in a $263 per month payment and an extra $4,920 in interest.

If you have private loans with variable interest rates and you can consolidate them into one private student loan with a reasonably low fixed interest rate then it may be worthwhile.

If you can't consolidate your private loans, use an aggressive plan to pay them off as quickly as possible, since they will often have interest rates that are higher than your federal student loans.

If You Cannot Make Your Payments...

You are a responsible person. You studied hard in college, brushed your teeth twice a day and recycled your plastic bottles. Now you want to be responsible and make your student loan payments. But despite your best efforts you have been unable to find a job, your job does not pay very well, or your employer "no longer needs your services." So what can you do if the bills keep coming in but the paychecks stop?

You will want to contact your servicer and explain your situation. If you do not have contact information for the servicer on your federal loans, then you will need to go to the National Student Loan Data System, *www.nslds.ed.gov* to find this information. Your servicer will explain your options and help you select the one that is best for your situation.

Whatever you do, do not ignore your servicer if you receive calls or letters about your payments. Federal student loans offer many options to make your payments more manageable. But you will not be able to take advantage of those options if you do not stay in touch with your servicer. Your student loans will not go away. They will only come back with much harsher penalties. Since there are so many ways to work with your servicer, no matter what your situation is there is no reason to avoid them. Instead, explain your situation and see what they can do to help.

Deferment

A deferment is a period of time where your servicer will allow you to stop making payments. You may be granted a deferment for various reasons, including:
-   Reenrolling in college at least half-time
-   Unemployment
-   Economic hardship
-   Military service

When I started graduate school I received a letter from my servicer letting me know that my loan payments were being deferred since I was enrolled in graduate school. It was a pleasant surprise, but looking back I should have continued making the payments anyway since I could afford them. It got tricky because as long as I was taking six credit hours my payments were deferred. One semester I only took three credit hours and I was suddenly ineligible for a deferment. You have to pay careful attention to the rules, and contact your servicer if you have any questions.

As long as you are enrolled in college at least half-time (based on the college's definition), including attending graduate school, your payments can be deferred. If you are unable to find a job or you experience another form of economic hardship (per federal restrictions) your payments may be deferred for up to three years. Your payments can also be deferred while serving on active military duty or for 13 months after you are released from active military duty if you were enrolled in college at least half-time when you were called to active duty.

Keep in mind that a deferment will simply extend the amount of time before you pay off your student loan debt. In fact, if you have an unsubsidized loan your interest will be added to your balance when your deferment period ends so you will owe even more money. For instance, if you defer payments for three years on a $20,000 unsubsidized loan with a 6% interest rate your loan will grow to $23,600 at the end of the deferment. Your new payments at the end of the deferment will be $40 more per month because of the extra interest that was added to your balance.

If you do not want to watch your loan balance get bigger over time then try to make payments anytime you can during a deferment. Even a partial payment is better than nothing. Just because your servicer says you do not have to make payments does not mean that you should not. Remember, your interest piles up during a deferment. You have to pay it eventually.

Forbearance

What happens if you are not eligible for a deferment but you still cannot make your payments? You may be able to get a forbearance. Forbearance means that temporarily you do not have to make payments or your payment amount may be reduced. Interest will accrue during a forbearance even if you have subsidized loans. Sometimes a forbearance is automatic – for instance, on the rare occasion when you have been affected by a disaster like a hurricane or flood, your servicer will give you a forbearance and let you know that you qualify.

In almost all other cases, you have to contact your servicer to request a forbearance. The forbearance period and your payment amount are determined by your servicer and it will be based on your particular circumstances. A forbearance may be renewed by your servicer.

With either a deferment or forbearance, continue to make your payments until your servicer lets you know it's been approved. Otherwise you may be penalized for missing payments or making late payments. You can confirm if your servicer has processed your deferment or forbearance by checking your loan status on NSLDS.

Guess what happens to your credit score if you just stop making payments or make them late? Your student loan servicer will report your late or missed payments to the credit bureaus which will negatively affect your credit score. The next time you need a loan, apply for a job, and so forth, you may be turned down because of a bad credit score. On the other hand, neither a deferment nor forbearance will negatively impact your credit score. So it's best to find out if you can take advantage of these options if you find yourself unable to make payments.

Regardless of your situation, if you do not have enough money left over at the end of the month to make your student loan payments there are options available. It is your responsibility to put forth the effort and contact your servicer to explain your circumstances. These programs are designed to help you avoid destroying your credit, but they are short-term solutions. As your interest accrues, or gets capitalized and added to the balance, the loans end up costing you more money in the long run. You still have the option of choosing one of the repayment plans mentioned earlier such as extended repayment, graduated payments that start smaller and increase, or even income-based repayment plans. When all is said and done, keep in mind that you borrowed money with the promise to repay it. You will be expected to do so.

Consequences of Not Paying

If you fail to make a payment for 270 consecutive days (approximately nine months) or more on a federal student loan, then you are considered to be in default. You want to do everything in your power to avoid default. With all of the options available to you for almost any financial situation you should be able to work out a way to avoid default, even if you are unemployed. If you know in advance that you will not be able to make your payments in full then you should contact your servicer as soon as possible to work out some arrangement. Even if you are already behind, you want to speak with your servicer before you reach the 270-day mark.

You cannot just bury your head in the sand and hope the issue will go away. Defaulting on your federal student loans carries serious consequences. Your university, the lender, the state government and the federal government may all take steps to get you to pay. For starters your lender will report your delinquent loan to the credit bureaus, which will trash your credit score, possibly preventing you from getting a loan, a job, an apartment, auto insurance, and more. The negative information will remain on your credit report for seven years. Any federal payments can be withheld to pay off your loan, including future tax refunds. There will also be additional fees and interest charges because of your failure to pay. As if that is not enough, your wages may also be garnished. That means your paycheck can be reduced as your employer sends a portion of your paycheck to your student loan lender. Also, you will not be able to get any student loans in the future until you clean up your current mess.

Not only do you owe what you borrowed, but you are also going to owe any interest that piled up while you were not paying. Keep in mind that you also pay interest on the interest, so it adds up quickly. Then you may also be charged collection fees since your inability to pay will result in a lot of money being spent by those trying to collect. Other legal action could also be taken against you. It is safe to say that you want to make every effort to pay your student loans, particularly federal student loans, or contact your servicer as soon as you realize you may not be able to make the payments on time.

One final warning--don't assume you can get rid of federal student loans through bankruptcy. The current law makes it extremely difficult to do so. In many instances you may not be able to wipe out private student loans either. If you have thousands of dollars of debt on credit cards and you have thousands of dollars of student loans and you just cannot seem to handle all of it you may be tempted to declare bankruptcy. The problem is that bankruptcy will destroy your credit for many years and you will still have to make student loan payments. Instead you will need to work with your servicer to make an arrangement for your student loans. Then take a good look at where the rest of your money goes and figure out how to get out from under the rest of your debt... even if it means getting a part time job to earn extra money for a while until you are able to eliminate some of the debt.

Eliminating Your Student Loans

Unlike a birthmark or that crazy tattoo you got right after that frat party your sophomore year, your student loans do not have to stay with you forever. In fact you probably want to get rid of your student loans as soon as possible... or do you?

In some ways student loans are like any other loan, the longer you hang on to the loan the more interest you will pay. And as long as you have that monthly payment it chips away at your budget. But unlike other loans you may have, the interest on your student loans is tax deductible. A tax deduction is not the same as free. In other words, you do not want to hang onto your loans *just because* you get a deduction. It does mean that you will probably want to pay off your other loans first, particularly if you have a fixed-rate federal loan. Variable rate private loans and those that your parents co-signed may be a different story. The interest may still be tax deductible, but the rates may be too high or you may just want to shake off that last bit of financial dependence with your parents so you can spend your money freely without getting dirty looks from them.

Let's start with the tax deduction. There are certain restrictions and income limits, but we will assume you are not going to hit those within the first few years after graduation. The deduction is not a huge amount of savings, but it certainly does help. Take a look at the following example:

Loan size: $20,000
Interest Rate: 7%
Payoff term: 10 years
Monthly payment: $232.22
Federal Marginal Tax Bracket: 25%

Total payments made in first year: $2,786.60
Amount of interest paid: $1,354.64
Amount of taxes saved: $338.66

The amount of money you save in this example by deducting your interest is the same thing as having a 5.25% interest rate with no tax break. Being able to deduct the interest does not make it free; it just makes it a little cheaper. So if you have other debts that have a higher interest rate, then you may want to pay those loans off first.

Once your other loans are paid off, you still want to try and pay off your student loans quickly because why would you want to pay almost $2,800 just to save $340 in taxes? In addition, as you pay down your loans over time the amount of interest gets smaller, which means you get to deduct less. For instance, in year five you only save a total of $223.37 in taxes. Figure 11-3 shows how much interest you pay each year and how much you can save in taxes assuming a 25% tax bracket.

Figure 11-3: Tax Implications of Student Loan Interest

	Total Payments	Amount spent on interest	Tax savings
Year 1	$2,786.60	$1,354.64	$338.66
Year 2	$2,786.60	$1,251.12	$312.78
Year 3	$2,786.60	$1,140.12	$285.03
Year 4	$2,786.60	$1,021.09	$255.27
Year 5	$2,786.60	$ 893.47	$223.37
Year 6	$2,786.60	$ 756.61	$189.15
Year 7	$2,786.60	$ 609.86	$152.47
Year 8	$2,786.60	$ 452.51	$113.13
Year 9	$2,786.60	$ 283.77	$ 70.94
Year 10	$2,786.60	$ 102.84	$ 25.71

Student loans are really part of your overall debt elimination strategy. I treat them separately to explain the differences--such as the multitude of repayment options, the severe consequences if you do not repay them, and the tax benefit that makes the interest rate lower than it seems. However, after understanding all of these unique characteristics it is time to look at paying off the loans as part of your big financial picture.

From the debt chapter you see that I recommend paying off your debt based on whichever loan you can pay off the quickest. There is something about the sense of satisfaction you get when you pay off your first loan or credit card. So go ahead and list your debts just like you are instructed in the debt chapter.

If you are having issues with your finances, facing a potential job loss, barely able to meet your payments, etc., and you have federal student loans, then you may want to automatically move your student loans to the bottom of your list of debts to pay off. Then contact your student loan servicer and see if they will work out a different repayment plan for you that involves smaller monthly payments or maybe even a deferment or forbearance if your situation warrants it. Again, the reason why you will pay your student loan off last under these circumstances is that student loans have much more flexible repayment options than your credit card company or your car loan company will allow. You want to pay off the difficult loans first and your easier loans last.

To Pay or to Play

You always want to have a nice balance between paying off your debt while still enjoying your life. If you focus entirely on enjoying life you are going to add to your debt, which will prevent you from enjoying the full potential of your earnings because of your high monthly debt payments. On the other hand, if you focus entirely on paying off your debt you will definitely end up in a much better position financially in a very short period of time, and you will be able to enjoy life that much more. But if you are completely miserable along the way then it may not really be worth it. You can create a balance if you stop going into debt (stop borrowing) and start paying more than the minimum payment.

As your income rises you can use some of your increased earnings to increase the amount you pay toward your debt, and use the rest of it to increase your lifestyle. After you pay off a debt you have that payment amount available each month. Take some, but not all, of that payment amount and add it to the next debt on your list, increasing the amount you pay toward that next debt. Now use the rest of the money to increase your lifestyle. Think of it as a reward for staying disciplined and eliminating a debt or completing a goal. Do this with each debt on your list and you could have them all paid off in just a few years.

Student loans, like any debt, do not have to be part of your life forever. Keep in mind that every debt you have equates to a certain amount of money every month that you cannot use for other things in your life. If you have three credit cards and a student loan with total monthly payments of $325 per month, that is $3,900 per year you are not able to spend on something important to you such as a really nice vacation or maybe even an investment to help you build wealth. In fact, once you consider the tax consequences of what you earn your $325 per month debt payment cancels out about $6,000 in annual income.

Think about that for a moment. If you can eliminate $325 per month in debt payments it is like giving yourself a $6,000 annual raise. If you make $30,000 per year that is a 20% pay raise! Once you start to realize that debt payments are the same as a pay cut and paying off your debt equates to a pay raise, your incentive to get out of debt begins to increase. As you eliminate your debt and free up your income you become an unstoppable force of potential. Okay, I may be getting a bit carried away, but the thought of giving yourself a big pay raise should get you excited.

The key to managing your student loans is to:
1. Understand exactly what you owe and to whom
2. Understand what makes student loans unique
3. Consider student loans as part of your overall debt elimination strategy
4. Look at your particular situation
   a. Decide where you are in your career
   b. Look at your current income and expected future income
5. Consider all of the potential repayment options and the consequences of each
6. Put together a plan to eliminate your debt
7. Contact your student loan servicer whenever you need help

Now, get ready to make some serious decisions so you can eliminate your debt and begin to really enjoy your income and your life.

Chapter 11 Action Steps

Your action steps are as follows:

1) Contact your college and ask for a list of all your student loans.

2) Visit *www.nslds.ed.gov* and compare your list of student loans with those provided by your college.

3) List all of your loans, payments, amounts owed, interest rates, and lender and servicer contact information.

4) Now you can see your total monthly payments and decide which repayment option is best for you.

Chapter 11 Summary

❑ You have to manage your student loans to keep them from managing you.

❑ It is critical to account for every loan so you know how much you have to pay and who you have to pay.

❑ There are various repayment options available to fit nearly every situation, including unemployment.

❑ You cannot use bankruptcy to eliminate student loans.

❑ Even if you are using a deferment or a forbearance, try to pay at least enough to cover your interest so your loan balance will not increase.

❑ The consequences of not paying student loans can severely damage your finances long term.

❑ Ultimately, you will pay off your student loans one way or another as part of your overall debt elimination plan.

12

Save, Invest, and Save Some More

With so many expenses coming at you sometimes it can be difficult to put any money away. Besides, even if you do have a few extra bucks, it's not enough to matter right? You probably don't even know what you should do with it either. Fortunately, we're going to make you a millionaire before you retire, and we're going to do it the easiest way possible. We'll call it the "Get Rich Steady" approach. Don't worry; if you are more interested in aggressive investing, we'll go over that too.

It's kind of ironic. If you just ignore your retirement and wait until your sixties, you'll be in bad shape. Most likely you won't be able to retire. On the other hand, if you set up the right kind of plan for yourself now, you should be able to ignore your retirement until your sixties, and you'll be in great shape. The only difference between a happy retirement and one that might not happen at all is careful planning. Of course, you don't really want to completely ignore it, but you can take a mostly hands-off approach if that's what you want.

So is that what this chapter is about? Retirement?

Not completely. Retirement is just part of your whole saving and investing "portfolio." let's start with why you should save, how you should save, and how the numbers work for you.

Why is saving so important? Just like paying off debt, savings gives us more choices. If you have money saved, you can go on vacation when you want. If you have enough money saved, you could buy a car whenever you find a great deal. Of course, if you have a lot of money, you could even retire when you want. The more you have saved, the more choices you have. You will also encounter situations where you had not planned to spend money. For instance, your car may blow a head gasket, or your television may accidentally fall off your wall. Having money in savings will help you to minimize your stress, and it will keep you from going into debt to pay for needed repairs (or replacement).

Before we get into too much detail about 401(k)s or IRAs, let's discuss some basic features of money. The first thing we should cover is the 80-10-10 rule. The 80-10-10 rule is nothing more than a guide to help you allocate your income. Basically, you should plan to spend no more than 80% of your money. You should also set aside 10% for savings and another 10% for charitable contributions. Why do we do this? It helps you have a more balanced life.

You see, too many people graduate college and use the 110% rule. This is a dangerous rule where the recent college graduate begins spending about 110% of what they earn. How is that possible you ask? We call that debt. First there is the credit card debt, then the car loans and then the mortgage. Before you know it, you have more debt than income and your payments are so high there is no room to breathe.

By learning to set aside 10% of your income for savings (or to use it towards paying off debt), you will immediately be on your way to living a comfortable life full of many choices and much less stress. In a few years you will be paying cash for your next car or buying a nice home with a large down payment or both. You will also have room in your budget to maneuver when an unexpected crisis occurs. Without the 10% savings, you could go 10 years at your job only to realize you have nothing more to show for it than a lot of extra bills coming in every month that keep you going back to your job. You could have done that without a degree!

The other 10% you should set aside is to allow you to contribute to a charity or charities. Perhaps you want to give to your church or your favorite cause (such as a children's hospital or an animal shelter). Maybe you would just like to be able to help a friend or colleague in need or give a large contribution towards the fight against cancer. Wherever you choose to give your 10%, I can guarantee it will help you feel better about going to work everyday, knowing you are contributing to something you believe in and are making a positive difference. Sometimes people think their contribution is too small to make a difference, but if you make $50,000 per year and contribute 10%, that's $5,000 for the year. There is not an organization I know that thinks $5,000 is insignificant.

Many of you are probably thinking, "I already save 10% of my income through a 401(k) at work." That's very nice, but the 80-10-10 rule only applies *after* you have saved through your retirement plan at work. In other words, the 80-10-10 rule applies to what is left over *after* you have money deducted for your retirement.

Retirement Plans at Work

So where do you begin? Let's start with your job. Does your employer offer any type of retirement account? Most employers offer a 401(k) plan, or something similar, such as a 403(b) or Thrift Savings Plan (TSP) account. This is usually the first place you should put some of your money. (The terms 401(k) and 403(b) refer to the section of the IRS code where the rules for these plans are located – Section 401, paragraph k, for instance.)

There are several advantages to using a plan through your employer. Most plans offer some sort of matching amount, based on your contributions. For instance, if you save 5% of your income in a retirement account, your employer might match it by adding an additional 5% into your account. In real numbers, if you earn $30,000 per year, and you put 5% towards your retirement plan, you will save $1,500 per year. If your employer offers a dollar-for-dollar match, your account would actually have $3,000 deposited for the year. That is an automatic 100% return on your money! If your account earns any type of return at all during the year, you will be in even better shape.

Of course, you need to ask your employer what type of plan they offer, and what the matching contributions are. Some employers only offer a 50 cents-to-the-dollar match. In this case, you would have to save 10% to get an extra 5% from your employer. In real dollars, if you make $30,000 and save 10%, you will have deposited $3,000 and your employer will have deposited an additional $1,500 in your retirement account. That is a 50% return on your money! Not as good as the last example, but still not a bad deal.

Another advantage is that your contributions come out before federal and state taxes (Social Security and Medicare are still taken out). If you are in the 25% federal and 5% state tax brackets, you are saving an additional 30% up front. The example in Figure 12-1 will show you the total benefits you will get from a pretax retirement account through work with a dollar-for-dollar match for the first 5%.

With Retirement Account		Without Retirement Account	
Income	$ 30,000	Income	$ 30,000
Contribution	1,500	Contribution	0
Tax Savings	450	Tax savings	0
Change in take-home pay	**- (1,150)**	**Change in take-home pay**	**0**
Matching	1,500	Matching	0
Savings outside of retirement account	0	Savings outside of retirement account	3,000
Savings Total	3,000	Savings Total	3,000
Net pay amount	**$ 28,850**	**Net pay amount**	**$ 27,000**

Figure 12-1: Benefits from Pre-tax Contribution with Company Match

As you can see by the example in Figure 12-1, by reducing your take-home pay by just $1,150 (less than $100 per month) you will have $3,000 in your retirement account! That does not even account for any interest you earn. Not a bad deal at all.

One of the first places you should park your cash is in a retirement account through work that has a matching contribution. One other advantage is that your contributions come out before you even see it. That's right. When you get your paycheck, the money is already in your account, so you don't have to have the discipline to deposit the money each month (or each pay period) yourself. Since you never actually see the money, you won't really miss it. Now that is a great deal. You could have more than $3,000 in your retirement account after one year, and you never even realized you were sacrificing anything!

There are a few little tips we should cover about your 401(k) plan. You have the ability to get to your money in the event of an emergency (such as a medical emergency or loss of a job), but this is a bad idea. If you do withdraw your 401(k) money before you retire, you will pay a stiff 10% penalty on top of your regular tax rate. In other words, if you withdraw $10,000 and you are in the 30% tax bracket, you will pay $3,000 in taxes (30% x $10,000) and pay a $1,000 penalty (10% x $10,000). Thus you only get to use $6,000 of your $10,000 that you withdrew. You don't have to be a math person to see how bad a deal that is.

You also have the ability to take out a loan from your retirement account for the purchase of a home (or a few other reasons based on tax law and company policy). Essentially you are paying interest to yourself for borrowing your own money. The only good part is that you are paying yourself the interest. Here is where it really gets tricky. Let's say you borrow $10,000 from your 401(k) and then you lose your job or you quit and take another job. You have to pay back the $10,000 immediately (within a very small time frame) or else you will be taxed and penalized as if you withdrew the money. Generally, I recommend you leave your retirement account alone if you can.

Finally, you have to be careful of the rollover IRA. Whenever you leave your employer, either by choice or by security guard escort, you have to decide what to do with the money that is already in your retirement account through that employer. In many cases, you are allowed to keep your money in the account through the former employer if you have worked for them for a certain length of time (such as three years) or if your balance is above a certain minimum. Whether you want to leave it or take it with you is up to you. Leaving it where it is would be the easiest approach, although if you continue to change jobs every few years, you might be dealing with too many accounts to keep straight. You should also check to see if you still have the same trading privileges you did as an employee. In other words, can you still move your money from one type of investment to another and log in or call to check your balance, etc? If not, you may want to move the money anyway.

So where do you put the money if you take it with you? Your best bet is either the rollover IRA or rolling it into your new company's 401(k) if they allow it. The rollover IRA is simply an IRA you establish to roll your money into from your current 401(k) plan. Simply choose an investment advisor or financial planner and tell them what you want to do. They can help you with the paper work to get the process started and move your money without incurring any penalties. Please be careful when you do this. If it is not properly handled as a "rollover", the company will cut a check to you, not the brokerage firm, and they will take out your income taxes. Then, if you do not have the money deposited into a retirement plan within thirty days you will owe the 10% penalty as if you withdrew the money. Even worse, if your company takes out federal taxes when they send the check to you, you will pay the 10% penalty on the portion that was taxed, unless you can also come up with that money to put into your new retirement account. Let's look at an example.

You leave your employer and have $20,000 in your 401(k). Instead of doing a rollover IRA, you simply tell your employer you want the money. They send you a check for about $13,000 (they held back $7,000, which is 35%, for taxes). If you immediately deposit the $13,000 check into a rollover IRA at this point, you will be assessed a 10% penalty on the $7,000 difference. Since the IRS knew you had $20,000 and now only deposited $13,000, they have to charge you this penalty. As you can see, it is very important that you rollover your money correctly. To make matters worse, if you don't get around to depositing your money until after the 30 days has expired, you will pay a 10% penalty on the whole $20,000. Plus you will have missed your opportunity to put the money into an IRA since there are restrictions on the amount that can be deposited in one year.

If you are self-employed, you have several other options available to you to save for retirement with pre-tax dollars. You can use the Keogh Plan, the Simplified Employee Plan (SEP) or the Solo 401(k). These three plans allow you to save pre-tax dollars from self-employment. You can usually save more through these programs than an IRA.

The best part is that even if you have a regular job working for someone else, and have your own business on the side (perhaps you are a wedding photographer or freelance artist on the weekends), you can still contribute from the amount you earn through self-employment. Let's assume you have maximized your contributions to your 401(k). If you earned $5,000 additional income from self-employment, the rules that apply for the Keogh, SEP or Solo 401(k) apply to that $5,000. In other words, with a Solo 401(k) you could save the entire $5,000 in your retirement plan and pay no federal income taxes on it. What a great way to fund your retirement.

Now that we've covered your retirement plan at work, where should you start parking your money? The next "category" that needs your attention is your emergency fund. What is an emergency fund you ask? Some people call it a rainy day fund. Basically it is money you have set aside in the event of an emergency.

Emergency Funds

Emergencies come in all shapes and sizes. If you get into a small accident you may need to pay the $500 deductible on your car insurance. Maybe your furnace will need to be replaced and it will cost $1,500. Perhaps you will get laid off from work and it may take a few months to find a new job. As you can see emergencies are unexpected events that drain our finances. Imagine if you have no money saved and you have to replace your furnace. What are you going to do, use a credit card? Do you really want to get back into that again? Let's say you lose your job. How are you going to make the credit card payment for your new furnace when you have no income? How will you eat?

Not to sound too dramatic, but you have to save at least $1,000. Everyone should have at least $1,000 in his or her savings account. From there you should build up your emergency fund to cover three to six months worth of expenses. Notice I said expenses, not income. We make more than we spend (hopefully). Also, we spend more than we need. What is three months worth of expenses? Well, rent or mortgage is needed, as well as other payments such as your car and insurance. You will also need to pay for utilities and food. What you do not need to worry about are things like savings, dining out, entertainment, etc. Sure, these things are nice, but you could probably forgo them if you had to.

So now you are contributing to your 401(k) at work, and you are saving money towards your emergency fund. You may be thinking there is not enough money left for anything else. Don't get too hung up on your emergency fund. If you save just 10% of your money towards an emergency fund, it will take you about two full years just to save three months worth of living expenses. My recommendation is to save the first $1,000, then focus on paying off your debt. After all, your living expenses will be lower if you do not have any debt payments.

Individual Retirement Accounts (IRAs)

After you are more comfortable financially, perhaps once your debt is paid off, you can begin investing on your own. You can invest outside of your 401(k) for your retirement, and you can actually invest just to make money. This is what we mean by making your money work for you. When you invest for retirement purposes, you can shelter your investments from taxes by using an Individual Retirement Account (IRA). An IRA is not an investment of its own, it is a type of investment.

An IRA could be a stock investment, a bond investment, a mutual fund, a certificate of deposit (CD), or a few other types of investments. You can choose between a traditional IRA and a Roth IRA.

The Individual IRA allows you to deduct the amount you contribute from your current taxable income. Thus, just like your 401(k), you will not have to "give up" as much money as you contribute from your current income. If you are in the combined 30% state and federal tax bracket, and you contribute $2,000 to your traditional IRA, you will save $600 in taxes this year (30% x $2,000 = $600). Even better, any gains you receive while your IRA is growing are not taxable. That means if your IRA increases from $10,000 to $20,000, you still pay no taxes. Once you retire and start withdrawing from your IRA is when you pay the taxes. You will be taxed as if the money you are taking out is regular income. In theory, by the time you retire, you will be in a lower tax bracket since you will not be working. Of course that will depend on what the current brackets are when you retire and how much money you take out of your IRA each year.

The Roth IRA does not provide immediate tax deferral like the traditional IRA does. In other words, if you are in the 30% tax bracket and you contribute $2,000 you will not save on any current taxes owed. The advantage of the Roth IRA is that you will not pay any taxes on your money when you withdraw it. Also, you will not pay any taxes on the money as your IRA grows (just like the traditional IRA). Basically, you have already been taxed on the money, so you are done paying the government their share.

So which do you choose? There are several factors that determine the best fit for your finances. The IRS has specific rules that govern how much you can earn and still be eligible to contribute. Assuming you do not make too much to be eligible, it really depends on how much money you have. As a rule of thumb, if you cannot afford to max out your IRA contribution, just stick with the traditional. That way you will either be able to contribute more, since you will save tax dollars, or you will still have spending money left over after you contribute. If you are easily able to maximize your IRA contribution, you may want to use the Roth IRA, since you will be able to withdraw more when you retire (since the Roth IRA will not be taxed when you withdraw). Here is an example.

To illustrate this with numbers, let's assume Matt contributed the maximum to a traditional IRA and Pat contributed the maximum to a Roth IRA. We'll assume their IRAs were both invested in the same mutual fund, so both of their accounts are worth the same amounts. If Matt withdraws $50,000 at retirement and he is in the 30% tax bracket, he will pay $15,000 in taxes and will only have $35,000 left to spend. If Pat withdraws $50,000 at retirement and she is in the 30% tax bracket, she will pay no taxes and will have the full $50,000 to spend. Again, this only applies assuming you can afford to maximize your contribution; otherwise you might as well use the traditional IRA.

There are special rules to consider with the IRAs. There are severe penalties if you withdraw your money early (before age 55 ½). You will pay a 10% penalty for withdrawing the money in addition to your regular income taxes. To make matters worse, if you withdraw a large portion of money from an IRA, it may actually push you into the next tax bracket. Assuming a 30% tax bracket, if you pull out $10,000, you will pay $1,000 in penalties and $3,000 in taxes. Thus, you are losing $10,000 in your retirement portfolio, and you only get $6,000 of it. Not a very good deal. If you pulled out enough to knock you into the next tax bracket, you would end up paying even more because a portion of that $10,000 may be taxed at 35%. As you can see, it pays to keep your money in your retirement plan.

The Rule of 72

Now that you have a better understanding of where to put your money and when, you may be asking "Why?" After all, you're a smart college graduate and you want to understand why money works this way. You're not content just letting me tell you what to do with it, right? The way investments grow is quite simple. It really boils down to the rule of 72.

The rule of 72 is an easy way to explain compound interest. When you put your money in a bank, for instance, you may earn about 3% interest (plus or minus, depending on the economy). If you put $100 in the bank at 3% interest, you can expect to have $103 in your account after one year. Big deal. But let's say you leave that $103 in the bank. The next year you will have $106.09. You earned interest on your interest! You earned 3% on the $3 interest you left sitting in your account. The extra nine cents may not seem like much now, but after 24 years, you will have about $200 in your account. That's right, you will have doubled your money in about 24 years. What if the interest did not compound? You would only earn $3 interest per year and it would take 33 years to double your money. You doubled your money nine years sooner just because of 3% that was compounding. What if you could earn 6% or 12% on your investment?

The rule of 72 says that if you divide the number 72 by the interest rate, the result is how many years it will take to double your money. Seventy-two divided by three is 24. It will take 24 years to double your money at 3%. Seventy-two divided by 12 is only six. If you were investing and earning 12% per year, it would only take you six years to double your money. This simple rule explains why the amount of interest we earn is so important.

Let's look at a few examples. Larry, Carrie and Mary are triplets who were each given $1,000 from their parents for Christmas on their 25th birthday. Larry puts his money in the bank and earns 3% interest. Carrie buys some corporate bonds and earns 6% interest. Meanwhile, Mary invests her money in the stock market and earns a 12% return annually. Forty years later, when the three are ready to retire, they check to see how much money they have. Larry is disappointed when he sees that he only has $3,315. Carrie is happy to see that she has $10,957 waiting for her after selling her corporate bonds. Meanwhile, Mary is able to do all the traveling she wants in her retirement with the $118,648 she has earned from the stock market! Look at Figure 12-2.

	Larry	Carrie	Mary
Interest earned annually	3%	6%	12%
Investment at age 25	$1,000	$1,000	$1,000
Age 31	$1,197	$1,432	$2,047
Age 37	$1,433	$2,051	$4,191
Age 43	$1,715	$2,937	$8,579
Age 49	$2,053	$4,206	$17,561
Age 55	$2,457	$6,023	$35,950
Age 61	$2,941	$8,625	$73,592
Age 65	$3,315	$10,957	$118,648

Figure 12-2: The Rule of 72

From the above example you can see that the interest rate makes all the difference in the world. Three people had the same amount of money to invest, and kept it invested and compounding for the same amount of time, but Mary, who was earning 12% ended up with more than 35 times the amount that Larry had earned! By the way, Carrie was no longer happy with her $11,000 after she saw how much her sister's investment was worth.

The power of compounding works best when combined with the power of time. You see, if the three of them would have checked their balances after 12 years, Larry would have about $1,433, Carrie would have about $2,051 and Mary would have about $4,191. There is still a significant difference among the three, but not as much as there was after 40 years. That is why you need to start thinking about your retirement now. Look at Figure 12-3 to see how compounding works over time.

What you should see in Figure 12-3 is that in the beginning, compounding creates a little bit of upward momentum during the first several years (through year 11). Then, the pace seems to pick up a little more (years 12 through 25), and then it really picks up the pace (years 26 to 33). Finally, look at how quickly the investment grows towards the end of this 40-year picture (years 34 to 40). Remember, this is just a one-time investment of $1,000 earning 12% interest per year. This example assumes no more money was added.

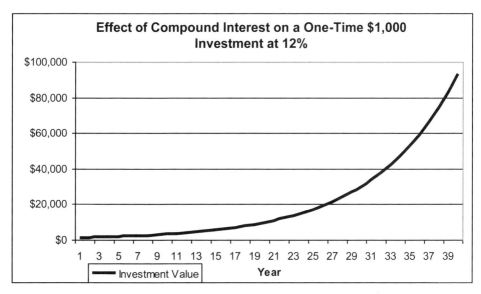

Figure 12-3: Compounding Interest Over Time

To get an even better picture of how compounding works, let's say the three siblings from the above example decided to save an additional $1,000 each year until age 65. After 40 years, Larry would have about $80,000, which is not bad, considering he only had to contribute a total of $40,000. Carrie would have about $175,000, which is really good considering she also contributed the same amount,

$40,000, over her working career. Mary, if you can believe it, would have over $1 million. That's right, she would have over $1 million and she only had to save a total of $40,000 over her working career. Mary is on her way to a very comfortable retirement.

Make Your Money Work for You

So now you have maximized your 401(k) and your IRA; you have your debt paid off; your emergency fund is set and you are finally ready to get into some serious investing on your own, the Wall Street way. Where should you begin? The best place to start is with a mutual fund.

Some of you are probably thinking, "Why start with a mutual fund? That's what I have my IRA invested in." Remember, the money you are investing now is nothing more than personal savings. This is the money you will use to supplement your retirement or buy a new car or a vacation home. You don't want to lose the first part of your hard earned savings right away in some oil scheme. I'm not talking about putting all of your money in a mutual fund, just the first part. Once you have a decent balance established, you can begin to move money into other riskier ventures. At this point you may want to look into real estate or individual stocks. Perhaps you would like to diversify into corporate or government bonds, depending on your age and risk tolerance. If you have enough money and you really like to play with fire you could even get into commodities and options trading.

Since there are entire books devoted to these riskier types of trades, I am not going to get into too much detail, but I will give you an overview of what they are. If this type of risky investment is definitely not for you, just skip to the next section, otherwise buckle up and keep your hands inside the vehicle at all times!

All Your Eggs in One Basket

We have all heard the expression, "Don't put all your eggs in one basket." This statement definitely applies to the world of investing. You always hear about people making millions of dollars by investing in individual stocks. Some people have made a fortune by sticking with one company throughout their lives (Microsoft, Wal-Mart, Google). So what is wrong with doing the same thing? Sure it's riskier, but people do it. Well, let's not forget about the people who invested all their money in Enron, FannieMae, or Kmart. If you like to gamble in Vegas with large amounts of money, perhaps putting all of your money into one stock is the way to go. Otherwise you want to diversify.

Why should you diversify? I'm not going to bore you with complicated graphs and statistics, but let's just say your risk of losing all of your money when you own stock from at least 13 different companies is way less than if you own the stock of just one. This is how it works. If you own, for the sake of simplicity, 20 stocks, with the same amount of money invested in each company, and two of the companies go completely out of business, you have only lost 10% of your money. If you would have all of your money in any one of these two companies, you would have lost 100% of your money. Now, assume that three more of the stocks stayed the same, five went up by 10%, five went up by 15% and the remaining five went up by 25%, your total "portfolio" would have still increased by 2.5%, despite the two companies that went under completely. The key to protecting yourself is to diversify.

So how do you diversify? If you try to buy the stocks from 20 different companies, it would cost you a fortune in transaction fees, besides the fact that you could only afford a few shares of each company. There is a much better way to diversify. We call them mutual funds. Mutual funds are basically a large "portfolio" of various investments. Since many people own pieces of a mutual fund, all of their invested money is used to buy a larger share of each investment and it allows the mutual fund manager to purchase many different types of investments to create a diverse investment vehicle.

There are many types of mutual funds. Some invest in stocks, some in bonds, others invest in both. There are also real estate mutual funds and many more. Each fund must follow a set of basic rules that only allows them to invest in certain types of assets. For instance, a growth mutual fund manager would be looking to purchase shares of companies that are expected to grow, so the growth fund will probably not have the stock from larger well-established firms such as General Electric or Coca-Cola.

To invest in a mutual fund use an investment firm, such as Charles Schwaab, Edward Jones, etc. They will set you up with an account after you invest a minimum amount and perhaps set an automatic contribution every month. The mutual fund manager takes your money, adds it to the money that is coming from other investors, and purchases either more shares of stock the fund already owns or perhaps shares of stock in companies that are new to the fund.

It is important to understand how the investment firm makes money. There are several types of fees that can be charged by mutual funds. There are no-load funds, low-load funds and load-funds. A load is another term for a fee. A load can be charged at the beginning of an investment or when you withdraw your money. If you are charged a front-load fee, for every dollar you invest, a few cents comes off the top right away for fees. So your investment has to earn a decent return just so you can break even. Back-loads are fees charged if you withdraw your money within a certain time period, usually seven years. For instance, you may be charged 5% if you withdraw your money within the first year, 4.5% during the second year, 4% during the third year, etc.

I prefer no-load funds, but keep in mind there are still fees involved, even in no-load funds; after all, the investment companies have to stay in business. They charge annual fees. You definitely want to stay away from funds that charge more than 2% in annual fees. After all, if you earn 8%, but pay 2% in fees, you are only really getting 6%. That is before any tax consequences are considered. The lower the fees the better. You should be able to find funds that charge fees of less than 1%. Of course, don't get so caught up in finding the lowest possible annual fees that you forget to see whether the mutual fund is right for you, or even if the fund has been performing well. What good is the lowest fee if the fund is losing money?

Okay, so let's talk a little more about mutual funds. There are several types of funds, which can be broken up into different fund styles. The styles really describe the styles of the managers of the fund. The style can be based on an index, investment strategy, a particular sector, company size, on bonds only, or a money market.

I prefer to invest in index mutual funds. An index fund simply holds a portfolio that represents a major index, such as the S&P 500 Stock Index or the Russell 3000. The advantage of the index fund is that the fees are usually lower since the manager does not have to work as hard to actively manage the fund. Since the goal is to imitate the index it is following, most of the guesswork is removed. There is no real statistical evidence that a professionally managed fund earns a better return for the amount of risk involved than an index fund.

Growth funds are managed to purchase stocks of firms that are expected to grow big over the next few years. Growth funds are riskier, because while they may return big, they may also fall big. Expect a lot of volatility with these funds as the value may go way up and way down from one year to the next. Value funds hold shares of companies the managers of the fund feels are undervalued in some way by the current market. They use all types of complex measurements and formulas, but the point is they feel the market is currently undervaluing the stock and they expect the market to eventually see the error of its ways, and bid up the price.

You can also look into sector funds. For instance, if you believe the health sector is on its way up, but are not quite sure which companies will be the winners, you could invest in a health sector fund, which will invest in the stocks of various firms within the healthcare sector. There are funds for almost every sector available.

Another way to choose stocks is based on the size of the companies. Company size is usually split between large-cap, mid-cap and small-cap funds. All this tells us is the size (or capitalization) of the company relative to the market. Most large-cap funds invest in companies with market capitalization of $8 billion or more, while mid-cap funds stay above $1 billion and small-cap fall below $1 billion. Large-cap funds are the least volatile, but also result in lower returns. Generally, small capitalization stocks are more volatile which means greater potential for loss but also greater potential for growth and returns.

Bonds

From your perspective, bonds are like loans in reverse. You give a large chunk of money to a corporation (say $10,000) and they make payments to you in the form of interest. At the end of the bond term, say 20 years, you get your principal back. One of the biggest drawbacks of purchasing bonds is that you lose the benefit of automatic compounding interest. You see, if you receive a payment from a bond every six months, you have to reinvest it at the same rate to enjoy the benefits of compounding. That is one of the reasons to invest in a bond fund instead of individual bonds. The bond fund manager can use the interest payments of the investors and collectively purchase more bonds.

Bonds come in all shapes and sizes. You can get everything from low-yield treasury bonds that are backed by the full-faith of the federal government to junk bonds, which are high-risk bonds issued by companies with credit problems. Government bonds include those issued by federal, state and local governments, while corporations issue corporate bonds. Bonds are rated according to their credit worthiness, much like we have our own credit score. Moody's and MorningStar are the two major credit-scoring companies in the bond market. The better a company's credit rating, the lower the risk they impose to the investor. In return, they will be able to get a lower interest rate.

In many ways bonds can work like stocks. Once you buy a bond, you are not necessarily stuck with it until maturity. You can sell the bond in a secondary market, similar to the stock market. In fact, you may have purchased it in this same market. Some people invest in bonds for a period of time, and then sell the bond to get money out for various things such as a vacation, education, etc. The question is how much can you get out of a bond when you sell it? That depends on the rating of the bond, the interest rates at the time and the coupon rate. As interest rates rise, the value of existing bonds falls. Why is that? If you have a bond that pays 5% interest, and new bonds are issued paying 10% interest, why would anyone be willing to buy your bond? They would want the new ones that are paying 10% interest. So how do you sell your bond in this case? You sell it at a discount. If you have a $10,000 bond and you sell it for less than $10,000 then you are selling it at a discount.

Let's say you have a 10% bond and the interest rates fall to 5%. Now the value of your bond just increased. After all, everyone wants to buy your 10% bond, since all the new ones are only paying 5%. In this case you will sell your bond at a premium. Your $10,000 bond will sell for more than $10,000.

Options

Buying and selling options is perhaps the closest thing to legalized gambling, next to state lotteries. With options big money can be made and big money can be lost. It is not uncommon for a person to make $20,000 in one day with options trading... and then lose $25,000 the next day. By no means should anyone try options trading based on the information I am giving you. If you want to seriously trade in options, there are appropriate books available that discuss the topic in detail. I am just giving you an overview.

Instead of purchasing a $50 stock, you could purchase an option, for say $5, which gives you the right to buy that same stock for $47. At first this may not make sense, because you paid $5 for something only worth $3 (If you would purchase the stock for $47 and sell it at $50, its current value, you would make $3, but the option cost you $5, so you essentially lose $2).

At this point your option is "out of the money," that is, it is worth less than its cost. You are probably wondering how this gives you any advantage... why not just buy the $50 stock? Well, if the stock increases in value by 10%, it is now worth $55. You could turn in your option at this point, pay $47 for the stock and sell it at the current market price of $55. You just made $8 profit, minus the $5 cost of the option, which means you netted a gain of $3. Big deal you say? Look at it this way. The stock price only went up 10%, but you made a 60% return on your money. How? You only invested $5, but earned a $3 return on your money.

To make this example clearer, let's compare two scenarios dollar for dollar. Matt and Pat each have $50. For simplicity's sake, let's ignore brokerage fees. Matt buys one share of ABC stock for $50. Pat buys 10 options, each $5, which give her the right to purchase the stock for $47 per share (total cost to each Matt and Pat is $50). If the stock's price increases by 10% to $55 and Matt sells his share, he made a total of $5, or 10% return on his money. Not bad Matt. Pat, on the other hand, exercises her 10 options and buys the 10 shares for $47 each and sells them for $55 each. Pat just made $30 compared to Matt's $5. Pat got a 60% return on her money. Sorry Matt.

You might be thinking, "Wow, that's amazing. Why doesn't everyone just buy options?" Two reasons. First, not every stock has an option attached to it. Second, the losses can be more significant if the stock decreases in value. Using the same example, if the stock decreases by 10% to just $45, then Matt loses $5 or 10% of his investment. Pat, on the other hand, loses the entire $50 since her options are now worthless (the stock costs less than the price at which her option allows her to purchase it). Pat lost 100% of her investment when the price dropped. Sorry Pat.

Dollar Cost Averaging

The easiest way to save money is to put away the same amount each month or each pay period. One of your regular monthly expenses should be your savings. When you invest in the stock market, you can expect stock prices will fluctuate. Dollar cost averaging is a way to let you invest without really worrying about what the individual prices of the stocks are at any given moment. Essentially you put the same amount of money in your investment every month (or pay period) no matter if the price is up or down. When the prices are up, the same $100 will buy you fewer shares, but at least your overall account has grown since the price increased. When the price goes down, it is like buying the same shares on sale.

Consider the following example. You invest $100 per month into the ABC mutual fund. The shares cost $20 each when you start investing so you own five shares. Next month you contribute the same amount, $100, but the shares fell to $10 each. Your account balance went down since the shares decreased, but now you are able to buy 10 shares at $10 each, so you own a total of 15 shares. When the price recovers to $20 per share the next month, your account balance is up to $300! You only contributed $200 so far and the price is the same as it was when you started, yet you have earned $100. Also, you will contribute $100 since you do so every month, which buys you five more shares.

Month	Your Investment	Cost per Share	Number of Shares Purchased	Total Shares Owned	Total Account value
1	$100	$20	5	5	$100
2	$100	$10	10	15	$150
3	$100	$20	5	20	$400
4	$100	$25	4	24	$600
Total	$400		24		$600

Figure 12-4: Dollar Cost Averaging

Next month the price increases to $25 per share, so your account balance is $400! This month your $100 savings will only buy four shares, leaving you with a total of 24 shares and an account balance of $600. Figure 12-4 makes this example clearer.

Chapter 12 Action Step

This action step is easy. It should result in more money at retirement and possibly lower taxes now. Review your workplace benefits. If your company matches your 401(k) contributions up to a certain percentage, then contribute enough to get the maximum matching contribution.   .

Chapter 12 Summary

❑ The 80-10-10 rule states that you should save 10% of your income and set aside another 10% of your income for charity, thus only spending 80%. This rule applies after you have contributed to your retirement plan through work.

❑ The rule of 72 states that to find out how many years it will take your money to double, divide 72 by the interest rate and the answer will be the number of years until it doubles.

❑ When interest rates increase, the price of existing bonds decreases and they sell for a discount.

❑ When interest rates decrease, the price of existing bonds increase and they sell for a premium.

❑ Options are high-risk investments that could lead to greater returns or greater losses.

❑ Compound interest allows you to earn interest on your interest. This allows your money to work for you over time.

❑ Dollar cost averaging is a systematic way to save the same amount of money every week, month, etc. without worrying about the daily fluctuations of the markets. You will minimize your risk of timing the market poorly.

13
A Financial Peripheral: Insurance

Just when you thought your life was getting easier, and now we start talking about insurance. It seems like every time you find a few dollars in your budget I come in and take it away. So what do you need to insure and how much should you spend? The one thing you'll notice is that the more you own, the more you end up paying in insurance. If you have a $30,000 car you will pay more for insurance than a $10,000 car. Insurance on a $300,000 home is more than on a $100,000 home.

That's the irony of spending. It costs more to insure more when you buy more. So what happens to that $300,000 home if a fire damages it and you do not have any, or enough, insurance on it? You are stuck with a mortgage payment and no home to show for it. Generally, if you have a loan, such as for a house or car, your lender requires you to have the proper amount of insurance to cover their interests. They don't want you to just default (stop paying) on the loan if something happens to your property.

Understand the Basics of Insurance Coverage

Insurance is a way of protecting you against large losses in the event your property gets lost, stolen, damaged or destroyed or you experience an illness or injury or if you are accidentally the cause of any of the above. That description covers most insurance.

If you understand that insurance is really a way of protecting you against large losses, you will be able to make better decisions on what type of policies to buy. Unfortunately, we have become spoiled over the years and we want everything to be covered by our insurance, with little deductible, if any at all. There is nothing morally wrong with this preference; it just costs us too much. Look at the difference on the premiums for your auto insurance based on a $100 deductible and a $500 deductible. You would have to get in an accident almost every other year to justify the difference.

Remember, when you follow the overall financial principles outlined in this book, you will be getting out of debt (if not already) and putting money back for emergencies and long-term desires. In doing so, you would not need a $100 deductible, because you would be able to handle at least a $500 deductible, or maybe more. By doing that, you will be able to save money on your insurance, allowing you to put more back for emergencies and long-term savings, which will allow you to increase your deductibles even more, etc. It is like an endless cycle of positive financial returns.

Life Insurance

How much life insurance should you purchase? It depends on your situation. If you are single and you own no real property, you don't need much life insurance, if any at all. The only reason to buy any life insurance now is to protect you in case you become uninsurable at a later date (contracting an illness or something similar). The main reason to purchase life insurance is to protect your loved ones... those who depend on your income... so they can continue on financially without you. For instance, if you are married and you own a home together, you would want your spouse to be able to continue living in your home even though your income is gone. If you have children, then you would want your spouse to be able to keep the house and also provide for your children's future (such as college expenses, etc.).

Even if you are not working, but are the primary caregiver to the children, will your spouse be able to stay home and care for the kids? Can your spouse afford to pay for someone else to care for your kids while he or she goes to work? These are issues you must consider when buying life insurance. The general rule of thumb says you will need between seven and ten times your annual income. So if you make $50,000 per year, your surviving dependents will need between $300,000 and $500,000 from your life insurance policy. Of course without children you will need less (and even less than that if you are not married). The more children you have, the closer you should get to ten times your salary (think about the rising costs associated with college).

Life insurance comes in many shapes and flavors, but it essentially boils down to two concepts: Whole-life and Term. Whole-life insurance covers you for your whole life (as long as you keep making your payments). There are dozens of varieties of whole-life as the insurance industry tries to repackage this concept to make it more attractive. The whole-life concept is usually tied to some type of investment that goes along with your policy. For instance, you would make a monthly payment for your insurance. A portion of the payment is for your insurance and a portion is for the investment. Over time you can expect your investment portion to grow. But there is a problem with whole-life insurance. First, it costs too much. Very few families can afford to buy enough whole-life insurance to provide between six and ten times their income in benefits. Second, most policies I have seen only provide the savings if you don't die. What's that you say? Doesn't everybody die? Yes. So there is no real point to whole-life.

Think about it. If your insurance is for $100,000 and you have an investment portion worth $80,000, the only thing your family gets when you die is the $100,000. What is the point of the savings? You would be better off investing separately from your insurance. Besides, the fees involved with whole-life are bad for you, but good for your agent's commissions.

A better alternative is term life insurance. How does term life work? Term life insurance works like your car insurance. You purchase it for a certain term. If you die during that term, your family gets the benefits. If you don't, you get to live longer. You have to consider what term makes the most sense. If you are just starting out, you may want a 20-year term policy. That gives you 20 years to pay down your debt and increase your savings (including your 401(k)) so when your term runs out, assuming you are still alive, your family will not need any life insurance benefits because you have wisely saved enough money to cover all of the expenses we just discussed a few paragraphs earlier.

A good way of looking at this philosophy is "buy term and invest the difference." Of course most of us do not do it this way, but nonetheless, if you buy term, you can use all the money you are saving in insurance premiums to pay off your house early and start a college fund for your children so you won't need the insurance benefit 21 years from now.

Health Insurance

One of the first decisions you will have to make when you start your job is which health insurance to choose, if you are fortunate enough to have choices through your employer. In many cases, especially with smaller companies, you do not have a choice. If you do have a choice, it may just be the amount of your deductible or whether you want prescription, dental or vision coverage. You will have to evaluate the costs of these additional insurance options and compare the costs to what you are already getting with your basic health insurance coverage. If you are already covered on your spouse's policy, rarely does it make sense for you to also get coverage for yourself, since you can only have something paid for once. Since, in many cases, it costs more to add your spouse to a policy than it does just to maintain your own coverage, it may actually make sense for each of you to have your own policy through your respective employers. If one of you loses your job, you can always add the other spouse since this is considered a life-change event (such as getting married, having a child, etc.).

Of course if one policy is significantly better than the other, maybe it still makes sense for both of you to be on one policy. Especially if the one policy covers a significant benefit you may need such as infertility coverage. Maybe one policy lets you choose your doctor and the other does not. That may be important enough to you to help sway your decision.

Whatever you do, please choose one of the health insurance options. You do not want to go without health insurance if you can help it. The presence of health insurance makes it necessary to have health insurance. If you go to the hospital for treatment and your health insurance will pay 80%, the treatment may cost your health insurance company $160 and you may pay $40 for a total of $200. That same treatment, if you do not have health insurance, may cost $500. How is that possible? Health insurance companies have a lot of power, and they have negotiated rates with 'in-network' providers. Thus, if the doctor or hospital is willing to be listed as 'in-network' they must agree to the negotiated rates. Someone without health insurance does not get the negotiated rate and must pay the full retail rate for the service, which is much higher.

If you work for a small employer, and you have health insurance coverage through your spouse, you may want to ask your employer if you can be compensated for not choosing to use their insurance. Why would they do this? Well, most employers pay between 50% and 75% of your insurance premiums. So if you would have to pay $200 per month for insurance, your employer is probably paying an additional $200 - $600 per month to subsidize your insurance. Assuming your employer's portion of the premiums are on the higher end, it may be cheaper for them to just pay you an additional $250 per month compensation for *not* using their insurance. They save money and you get more pay. It is a win-win situation. My wife and I got this deal with her very first job. It more than made up for the additional amount I paid for insurance through my employer by adding her to my insurance.

Healthcare Flexible Spending Accounts (FSA)

While this is technically not insurance, it falls within this section. While you are choosing your insurance, you can also elect to have a portion of your paycheck taken out pre-tax, which you can use to pay for medical expenses not covered by insurance. Here is how it works: If you have $600 taken out of your paychecks for the year ($50 per month) then you will not pay taxes on that $600 (which will save you about $150 in taxes). The first $600 you spend on medical expenses not covered by insurance, such as your co-pay, your deductible, contact lenses, acupuncture, etc. you can submit to your FSA plan and they will reimburse you for it. Basically you saved taxes on money you were going to spend on medical expenses anyway.

The only disadvantage is that any money you do not use by the end of the plan year you will forfeit. So if you set aside $600 you will save $150 in taxes, but if you only use $300, then you actually would have lost money. I realize this is a guessing game, but you may be able to estimate your expenses by looking at your deductibles and figuring how much you will spend at the dentist, optometrist, family doctor, etc. (In my case, if I have a little extra at the end of the year, I usually buy a year's supply of contacts or a new pair of glasses with it so I have never really lost any of my FSA money.) If you are planning to have a major medical expense such as laser eye surgery, you may want to put at least enough to cover the surgery (minus what your insurance may pay) so you can at least save some money in taxes to help offset the cost. Be careful, most cosmetic surgeries are not covered. For more information see *www.flexadministrators.com* or check out IRS Publication 502 at *www.irs.gov.*

Disability Insurance

Let's face it. At your age you are much more likely to get sick than become disabled, so that is why health insurance is your number one priority. On the other hand, at your age, you are much more likely to become disabled than die, so disability insurance may actually be more important than life insurance.

Disability insurance comes in both long term and short term. A short term disability policy may be used during a pregnancy that requires bed rest or during a recovery period after a surgery. Long term disability is used when you are stricken with a debilitating disease or suffer a serious injury that will keep you from working for a long time, or even the rest of your life.

Disability insurance usually protects about 60% of your income, up to $100,000 per year. If you were to become disabled, your family would not get any life insurance (since you have not died), but you may not be able to work, so they are still without your income. You want to purchase '*your occupation*' protection. The terminology may vary somewhat, but there is '*any occupation*' protection and '*your occupation*' protection. '*Any occupation*' protection sounds better, but it basically means if you cannot perform any job, then you are covered. If you are a surgeon, and you qualify to serve fries, you may not qualify for benefits since you can perform *some* job. On the other hand, with '*your occupation*' coverage if you can no longer perform your own job, you will be covered and will receive benefits.

With most policies you will have to consider the elimination period, which is the time between your disability (when the injury or illness occurred) and when your benefits begin. Usually there will be at least a 30-day elimination period. Of course, the more you have saved in an emergency fund, the longer you can stretch your elimination period and the more you can save on your monthly premiums. You also want to look at what the benefit period is (how long will you receive payments). There is a cap on most policies so see which one best fits your situation. Balance these two considerations with monthly premium and monthly benefit and you should be able to find the policy that best fits your needs.

Property and Casualty Insurance

Property and casualty insurance mostly encompasses when something happens such as an auto accident, a house fire, theft, etc. The two most common types are auto and homeowners (or renters) insurance.

Auto Insurance

Auto insurance is separated into different categories:
(1) Bodily Injury – pays for medical expenses for you and others.
(2) Property Damage – pays for other people's property that you damage.
(3) Comprehensive – pays for damage to your car other than that caused by a driving accident (tree falls on your car, catches on fire, etc.).
(4) Collision – pays for damage to your own car in the case of an accident.
(5) Medical payments – pays for medical bills for you & any passengers, no matter who caused the accident.
(6) Extras include towing & road service, uninsured motorist coverage, no-fault (or PIP) and death & dismemberment.

Do not pay for towing or death & dismemberment coverage. They are not worth their costs. Once your car is worth less than $2,000 there is no reason to pay for collision and comprehensive coverage. You won't get enough money out of a claim at that point.

To help keep your costs down:
(1) Increase your deductible to at least $500. Unless you have one accident every year, it's almost always cheaper to have the higher deductible.
(2) Never file a claim for less than $750. Your rates usually increase, and since your deductible is $500, it's not worth it (unless there is a personal injury involved).
(3) Ask for some of the standard discounts:
   i.   Multi-car or multi-policy (home and car) or both
   ii. Antitheft equipment
   iii. Air bags
   iv. Anti-lock brakes
   v.   Low mileage (if you do not drive much)
   vi. Good driving record

When you have insurance on your car, if you let a friend drive the car (on occasion, not as the full time driver), your friend is covered by *your* policy.

When reading an auto insurance policy, the numbers may look like: 40/60/30, meaning:
- ❏ $40,000 for bodily injury per person (maximum)
- ❏ $60,000 per bodily injury per accident (maximum)
- ❏ $30,000 coverage for property damage (maximum)

When comparison-shopping for auto insurance, be sure to compare the same coverage for each company. Ask what happens to your rates after one accident, and after any points or moving violations (such as a speeding ticket). Some companies start with low rates but increase your rates substantially after just one claim or speeding ticket.

Homeowners and Renters Insurance

Homeowner's insurance comes in six flavors. They are HO-1, 2, 3, 4, 5, 6, and 8. HO-1 is a basic homeowner's insurance. HO-2 covers a more broad range of claims. HO-3 (most common) covers everything that could happen to your home except specific exclusions and covers certain things that can happen to the belongings inside your home. HO-5 covers almost everything that can happen to your home *and* your belongings, unless specifically mentioned (such as nuclear accident, war, and floods). HO-4 is renter's insurance, HO-6 is for condominium owners, and HO-8 is the worst coverage possible as it only covers current value, not full replacement value.

Most policies will cover your personal belongings up to half of the amount covered for the house. In other words a $100,000 policy on your home would cover up to $50,000 in personal belongings. If you wish to cover expensive items such as jewelry, fur coats and antiques, you normally must add a rider to your policy to specifically include these items.

Make sure you purchase at least 80% coverage. This is called the 80% rule. With 80% coverage you can get the full replacement of your home (up to the amount of your coverage), while anything less means you only get a percentage. For example: You have a $100,000 house with 70% coverage. If your house incurs $20,000 worth of damage, you will get $14,000 (70%). If you had 80% coverage you would have received the entire $20,000, because it still falls within the range of 80% of your total coverage. It may not make sense, but that's the way it is.

Also, buy replacement value, not market value. Replacement value will actually pay to replace your belongings, while market value will pay to replace what the belongings were worth when they were lost, which includes age, wear and tear, etc. (For example, a $1,000 sofa may only have a market value of $500 after a few years).

Your policy not only protects you in the case of damage to your home, but it also offers you protection from personal liability. If someone slips on your property or your tree falls on someone's car, your policy will cover you, up to some maximum limit.

If you rent, you should seriously consider buying renter's insurance. Not only will it protect your belongings (television, bike, small appliances, clothes, etc.), but it will also offer you some liability protection (just like a homeowner's policy) as well.

If you live in a flood plain, you should purchase flood insurance. Regular insurance policies do not cover flood damage.

If you have to file a claim, document your loss as much as possible. Make a list with descriptions and use any receipts or photos available.

Avoid the Wrong Kinds of Insurance

So what are the wrong kinds of insurance? Let's start by describing my approach on how to determine what makes one kind of insurance wrong. I have two criteria that I use to determine whether insurance is wrong or not. 1) It costs too much for what you are getting and 2) You don't need it. That's basically it. Certain types of insurance simply cost too much for what you are getting in return. Extended Warranties are a prime example. I know it may be a stretch to classify extended warranties as insurance, but basically you are buying a policy that will cover your losses in the event that something happens to your personal property. That pretty much describes property insurance.

Extended Warranties

So what is wrong with extended warranties? They offer peace of mind after all, don't they? Yes, but how much is piece of mind seriously worth? Let's take an example. You buy a washer for $500 and a dryer for $450. You just spent $950. You also paid taxes and possibly a delivery fee. For sake of argument let's just say you spent $1,000 total. Now, you can purchase an extended warranty for your washer for $150, which covers you for three years and one for your dryer for just $100 more that also covers you for three years. So you just increased the total cost for your washer and dryer by 25%. Instead of spending $1,000, you just spent $1,250.

Of course if you also buy the warranty for your refrigerator and dishwasher, etc. you could practically bankrupt yourself. And, all you get out of it is three years. Based on the 25% premium they charge for all these warranties, the only way you could come out ahead is if more than one-fourth of your appliances break down in the first three years. If that happens, then God is trying to send you some kind of message.

Extra Life Insurance Through Your Employer

What is wrong with purchasing life insurance through your employer? Well, for most employers a portion of your life insurance comes free. If not, there is usually an amount equal to your salary that is very reasonably priced, and you may want to purchase it. However, when your employer offers you the chance to purchase additional life insurance, look closely at the cost. It is almost always cheaper to purchase a separate policy on your own, outside of work (unless you have a serious pre-existing condition and cannot purchase life insurance on your own). Plus, you cannot take the policy with you when you leave that job. Think about it. If you purchase a 10-year term life policy on your own, not only will you pay less than half of what you would have to pay through work, but also that policy stays with you even if you quit or lose your job.

Whole Life Insurance

I know we discussed this before, but do not buy life insurance that has an investment attached with it. Don't do it. You would be better off burning dollar bills to stay warm in the winter. At least that way you are not paying commission to someone who either cannot do math very well or does not have your best interest in mind. Remember, if you buy term insurance (15-year or 20-year level would be good), you will save a lot... a whole lot... of money. If you seriously try to purchase up to 10 times your salary in whole life, you won't have any money left over to buy food. Now, you can use the money you saved to pay off your debt (see Chapter 10) and invest the money for your future (see Chapter 12). That way, when you reach the age when your term policy runs out, you will be self-insured. You will have enough in investments to cover all the things that usually need to be covered by insurance.

Mortgage Insurance

Unless you are in a situation where you are required to purchase mortgage insurance by your lender, do not purchase it. Think about it, all you are doing is buying insurance to protect the bank in case you are no longer able to pay them. Why should you pay for insurance to protect them? They have money. Let them protect themselves. What you should be doing is putting money away into an emergency fund to cover you in case you lose your job. What happens if you become disabled and cannot work? Refer to our previous discussion about disability insurance.

Long-term Planning Insurance (under the age of 50)

At this point, you are way too young to purchase long-term care insurance (LTC). LTC will protect you and your assets in case you have to go into a nursing home or you need to be cared for by a nurse at home. At this stage in your life, you do not have many assets that need protected. You will pay so much in the way of premiums over the next 20 years that you are better off saving that cost and using it towards some of your more immediate needs. When you reach age 50, you can take another assessment of your situation to see if LTC makes sense.

Accidental Death and Dismemberment Insurance (AD&D)

Seriously. Have you ever looked at these policies? "If you lose your left leg and your right eye then you are entitled to…" Who gets in these types of accidents anyway? The way these policies are designed by insurance companies is to use their actuaries to determine some seriously unlikely situations and then they cover you for these specific scenarios. Don't buy it. What you should have is long-term disability insurance, and maybe a very good lawyer if one of these types of accidents happens at work or because of someone else's negligence.

Cancer Insurance and Critical Illness Insurance

These policies are similar to the AD&D policies. There are very specific scenarios that are covered and very limited coverage at best. They only cover for specific illnesses, and only cover specific expenses for these illnesses. On top of that, they only offer up to certain maximum dollar coverage in most cases. And as with almost all insurances, any preexisting condition you may have is not covered. You can't buy life insurance for a dead person, and you can't buy critical illness insurance for a critically ill person. Your best bet is to have a good, comprehensive health insurance plan (usually through your employer if you are not self-employed).

Despite my ranting, I am not against the insurance industry. I simply understand that insurance agents are sales people, the same as stockbrokers are sales people and car dealers are sales people. In many cases the individual sales person starts thinking more about their commissions than about the person they are trying to assist. Their goal is to get some of your money to feed their family. Your goal is to keep more of your money to feed yours. So keep in mind that some of the policies listed above are the ones that provide the best commissions for the sales people which is why they try so hard to sell these policies to you.

Chapter 13 Action Step

As always, I am concerned about helping you save money. So your action step is to review your insurance policies (auto, life, health, etc.) and make sure you are following the principles in this chapter to get the best coverage at the best rates. Since I also want to make sure you are well protected, get renters insurance if you don't have it already! It is relatively inexpensive, but will help you recover any losses if something happens to your apartment or the stuff in it.

Chapter 13 Summary

❏ Insurance is a way to protect your assets, including your income, in the event of an illness, accident or disaster.

❏ The major types of insurance include auto, home (or renters), health, life and disability.

❏ Life insurance can be divided into term insurance and cash value insurance.

❏ Term insurance is only good for a certain term (such as 10 or 20 years). It carries no other value except to protect your family in the event of your death. It is much less expensive than cash value insurance.

❏ Cash value insurance (also called whole life insurance) has a cash value attached to it. It combines your insurance and some type of investment. Cash value is much more expensive than term, but it lasts your whole life. If you die, your family will only get the insurance portion, not the invested amount.

❏ Your auto insurance may include collision, comprehensive and medical. Collision covers property damage you cause to another vehicle or someone else's property. Comprehensive covers damage to your car. Medical covers any medical costs for you, your passengers, or anyone injured because of you.

14
A Life Less Taxing

I had to ask myself, "How could I make a chapter about taxes fun?" I don't think anybody actually looks forward to paying taxes. That's not to say we don't do it, but it just takes away a large part of what we earn. I don't know if I can really make taxes fun, but I can at least take some of the mystery out of the tax code and make the whole process seem much less scary.

We have many different levels of taxation. The first portion of taxes we notice are the federal taxes that come right off the top of our paychecks. You may also notice your state income taxes (unless you live in one of the states that do not have income taxes), and then there is social security. By the way, your social security taxes are about the same as your state taxes in many cases. Just think, so much of your hard earned tax dollars are right now being fed into some slot machine in Vegas by a retiree. Anyway, all of these are called payroll taxes. We will discuss them more deeply in just a moment.

We also pay other taxes, which are called use taxes. When you purchase an item in most states you will pay a sales tax. Sales taxes are essentially use taxes. You pay taxes because you used something. You also pay plenty of taxes on your telephone bill, electric bill, gas bill, and so on. The gasoline that you buy at the pump already has taxes built into the price, so even though it doesn't seem like you are paying taxes on your gasoline, you are. You have probably heard the expression that the only two sure things are death and taxes. Now you know why. Someone once said, "If you can see it, touch it, feel it, taste it, hear it or even think of it, they can tax it." Consider it a cost of doing business in the United States.

Understand Your Taxes to Make Them Less Scary

For most people just starting out, taxes are not that complicated. All you have to do is report how much money you make and fill in about four or five other lines on your tax return and pay your taxes. You don't even have to calculate how much you earned because your employer sends you a statement in the mail at the end of the year that says how much you earned and how much you have already paid in taxes (the form is called your W-2). Now, if you want to learn how to minimize the amount you pay in taxes, that's where it starts to get a little tricky. Not to worry, because we'll go through just about every step you need in order to complete your tax return. We will also discuss ways to minimize your tax liability.

The first question most people ask is, "do I have to fill out a tax return." The answer: "Hopefully." If you do not need to fill out a tax return, it would be because you did not make enough money that year. How much is enough? Well, that too changes each year to account for inflation, or any tax law changes. Visit *www.irs.gov* or refer to the "Do You Have to File" section of the Form 1040 Instructions.

The next question people ask is, "Do I have to file a tax return if the government owes me money?" The answer: "Yes." The IRS is not interested in keeping your money (just their fair share). Regardless of whether you owe tax dollars or if you are eligible for a refund, you have to file your tax return, and you have to file it on time (by April 15th). There are exceptions to filing your return on time, but you have to file an extension (IRS Form 4868). However, even if you are granted an extension, you still have to pay any taxes owed. Your payments are not extended, only the filing of your return. Now, you may ask, "How do I know how much I owe if I haven't completed my tax return." The answer: "You don't." Kind of funny isn't it? You should have an estimate and pay accordingly. Your best bet is to over estimate so you won't pay any interest (or penalties in some cases). In that case, when you do file, you will get back any over payments.

So, when should you file your taxes? Before April 15th. If you are owed a refund, I suggest you file your return as soon as possible. The sooner you get your money back, the better. While you're at it, you should request a direct deposit so you'll get your money even faster, within two weeks in some cases. There is space at the bottom of your return to fill in your bank information. You can refer to the sample check in Chapter 4 if you need help finding the routing and bank account numbers.

If you owe money, hold off as long as possible before sending any money. If you file electronically, you can file your return whenever it is convenient; yet specify the exact date that the money should come out of your account. In other words, you could file in late January, but not have your money sent to the IRS until April 15th. Just don't forget to make a note of that in your checkbook. You don't want the IRS to get an "insufficient funds" notice when they go to get your tax money from your account.

For the record, your employer has until January 31 to send out your W-2. The W-2 is the form that shows how much you made for the year, how much you paid in taxes, how much you put in your retirement account, etc. If you work as an independent contractor, and are not actually an employee of the firm that pays you, they will send you a Form 1099 instead. In most instances, if you are receiving a Form 1099, the firm you worked for was not taking any taxes out of your paycheck (hopefully you were setting money aside or making estimated quarterly payments).

You cannot file your taxes until you have all of this information. Notice that I said they had to *send* it by the 31st of January. That means you might not receive your W-2 until the second week of February (hopefully it won't take that long). If you changed jobs at any point during the previous year, you will receive one from each employer. If you have not received your W-2 by the second week of February, you should contact your employer. It is your responsibility to have the information and to file your taxes on time.

While you are waiting, if you have your last pay stub of the year (it may have been received in January) you can see in the "Totals" column how much you made, and how much you paid during the year. If you have contacted the employer at least twice and the April 15th deadline is approaching, use the information from your final pay stub and include a letter to IRS explaining that you contacted the employer on such and such a date (or dates) and they still have not provided your W-2. All of this applies to your bank or brokerage account statements as well. They should have sent something that indicates how much you made in interest or dividends for the year. You will have to include this information on your tax return as well.

Learn to Fill out the Basic Tax Form

Now it's time to get our hands dirty. Let's talk about actually filling out a tax return. So what form do you choose, 1040, 1040A, 1040EZ? The basic form for individual taxpayers is the Form 1040. The other forms are just variations, some are easier and some are harder. For now, unless you are self-employed, you can ignore all of the other tax return forms. If you are self-employed you will be using a Schedule C in addition to your 1040.

The easiest Form is cleverly titled Form 1040EZ (see, even the IRS can have a little fun). Certain restrictions limit who can use this form, but essentially it is for people who make less than a certain amount of income and have limited deductions. The Form 1040A is more complicated, but only a little. There are not as many restrictions on this form as the 1040EZ, but there is still an income limit, a smaller list of credits that can be taken and a select list of income sources (such as wages, pensions, etc.). For most recent graduates, the 1040EZ or the 1040A will be the most appropriate. The longest form is the regular Form 1040. It is definitely the most complicated of the three, but there are no restrictions on who can use this form. If you are going to take itemized deductions (such as mortgage interest), or if you make above a certain amount of income, you must use this form.

Now you have to decide if you are filing as single, married filing jointly, married filing separately or head of household. If you are single and you have a child and you meet certain other criteria, you may be able to file as head of household. This is by far the most lucrative status, as far as taxes are concerned. If you are single and you have no children or you do not meet the requirements for head of household, you must file as single. If you are married, you must decide whether to file separately or file jointly. Joint filers simply add their incomes together and use the married filing jointly column on the tax tables to determine their tax. Taxpayers who are married filing separately simply fill out two separate tax returns, one for each spouse.

Of course, if you file married filing separately you cannot both claim the same deductions. For example, if you have one child, you can't file separately and each claim the same child as a deduction. It almost always costs more in taxes to file as married filing separately. Sometimes if you have large medical expenses or some other type of similar deduction that has an income floor, it may pay you to file separately. Also, if one spouse makes more than twice what the other makes, it may pay to file separately. In many cases if a couple is separated, but are not yet divorced, they will each file separately. If you are unsure which way you should file, fill out the tax return both ways and see which way costs the least amount in taxes. You can always switch the following year if necessary.

Before you fill in your income, let's define a few key words.

❏ Total Income – Also called Gross Income, includes all of your income from your job, small business investments, interest or dividends received, etc.
❏ Adjusted Gross Income (AGI) – Total Income, minus certain deductions, such as 401(k) or IRA contributions. Your AGI is used to determine your eligibility for certain credits and deductions.
❏ Taxable Income – AGI minus certain other deductions and personal exemptions. Your Taxable Income is used to calculate your *tax liability* or *Total Tax*. You look up your Taxable Income on the tax tables to see what you owe.

Okay, so you have to fill in your Total Income. You should at least be happy for a moment as you see how much you made for the year (until you start wondering where it all went). From here you will take out your deductions and calculate your AGI. Now you get to take your personal exemptions, which includes yourself, your spouse (if you are married filing jointly) and your children (pets do not count). For a brief moment it actually feels like getting married and having children were good ideas (financially speaking, of course).

Your next calculation will tell you what your Taxable Income is. If you compare this number to your Total Income you will definitely feel somewhat relieved. Refer to the tables in your taxpayer instructions and see how much tax you should have paid for the year.

Essentially you look and see which column to use (single, head of household, etc.) and follow that column down until you find the range that has your taxable income. Find your taxable income on the table (it will be within a range) and line it up with your filing selection and see what your taxes owed will be. Write this amount in the Tax Owed box and subtract that amount from what you paid. If what you paid is a bigger number than what your liability is, you will get a refund! If it is smaller, you will owe. It is really that simple.

I would recommend using a spreadsheet if possible, or at least a calculator. A spreadsheet is better because you can see exactly what you entered, which is important if you make a mistake somewhere.

A word of caution: If you owe tax dollars, do not pay with a credit card. I repeat, do not pay your taxes with a credit card. Even if you always pay your card off at the end of each month you are still losing out. If you remember from the credit card chapter credit companies receive a small percentage of each transaction. The IRS will not allow them to receive this percentage, which means you will have to pay it. Essentially you will have to pay an additional 2% on your taxes. It might not seem like much, but money is money. And it is doing you a whole lot better in your pocket than in some bank's vault. If you owe $500 in taxes, you will pay an additional $10. That's $10 that you could use for something better. Just have the money taken directly out of your checking account or send a check.

Deductions, Credits and Deferrals

So, what are the differences among a deduction, a credit, and a deferral? Well, they are all three completely different, but they have one thing in common. They all reduce your current tax bill. Next to earning less money, the only way to pay less in taxes (legitimately) is to use one of these three tax items (See Figure 14-1 for a summary of the three).

Deductions

Tax deductions are a great benefit. For instance, if you are eligible to take a deduction for business travel, it can help offset the amount of taxable income. You save an amount equal to your marginal tax rate times the amount of your deduction. For instance, if you have a $500 deduction and you are in the 25% tax bracket, you will save $125 (500 x .25 = 125). Deductions actually reduce your taxable income. If you made $40,000 and you have a $500 deduction, you will be taxed on $39,500 of income. Let's say on $40,000 your tax liability would be $5,000. Then your tax liability, after the $500 deduction, would be $4,875 since you are only taxed on $39,500.

The most common deduction is the standard deduction (discussed earlier). If you choose to itemize your deductions, the most common is the mortgage interest deduction. You can also deduct certain business expenses, as well as medical expenses, interest paid on student loans, taxes paid, certain charitable contributions, certain job expenses, losses from theft or destruction, and many other miscellaneous expenses. They are all restricted based on certain IRS rules. For more information refer to IRS Publication 17.

Credits

Credits are even better than deductions. A credit actually reduces your tax liability dollar for dollar. For instance, using the above example, if you made $40,000, your tax liability would be $5,000. If you can take a $500 tax credit, your taxable income would still be $40,000, but your tax liability would only be $4,500 ($5,000 - $500 = $4,500), because a credit directly reduces your *tax liability*, not just your taxable income!

Some of the common credits include the Child and Dependant Care Credit, Child Tax Credit, Earned Income Credit, and the Adoption Credit. For more information on credits, see IRS Publication 17.

Deferrals

Deferrals are very similar to deductions. They operate in the same way, by offsetting your taxable income. The most common type of deferral is by contributing to an IRA or 401(k) retirement account. Using the above example again, if you made $40,000, and contributed $2,000 to your 401(k), your taxable income would be $38,000, and your tax liability would be reduced by $500 ($2,000 x .25 = $500). Your total tax liability would be $4,500, instead of $5,000. The reason it is called a deferral is because you will pay taxes on this income when it is distributed from your retirement account years from now. In other words you are deferring these taxes until later.

	What does it do?	Example: 25% tax bracket
Deductions	Reduces your taxable income. You save a percentage of the deduction from what you pay in taxes.	$500 deduction = $125 in tax savings. ($500 x .25 = $125)
Credits	Reduces your tax liability. You save the dollar amount of the credit from what you pay in taxes.	$500 credit = $500 in tax savings. (Tax bracket does not matter: $500 = $500)
Deferrals	Reduces your current taxable income. Taxes are paid later, when funds are withdrawn and used.	$500 deferred = $125 in tax savings for current tax year. Taxes paid later.

Figure 14-1 Description of Tax Reduction Options

Explore the filing options, including electronic filing and paid preparers

Perhaps some of you noticed that your parents paid someone else to handle their taxes. Maybe math just isn't your thing, and you'd rather have someone else do the calculations for you. Before you pay someone else, consider your other options. You could purchase tax software, which is very easy to use, or you could prepare your taxes yourself.

Assuming that your taxes are not very complicated, you could just file them yourself. What do I mean by not very complicated? Well, let's say that you just graduated from college, you do not have any investments, other than your 401(k) at work, you did not inherit any money this year and you do not receive any money from a trust fund (wouldn't that be nice).

If that sounds like you then there is no reason to pay someone else to do your taxes. You can complete them in less than one hour. All you will need will be your W-2 (if you had more than one job then you should have a W-2 from each employer), a statement that says how much interest you paid in student loans, if you have any (Sallie Mae borrowers can log onto their website and print a form that states how much they paid in interest) and your bank account statement that shows how much interest you earned this year. Other than that you will fill in a few extra lines on your return (personal exemption, standard deduction amount, etc.) and you are done. If you're lucky, you'll be getting a refund.

If you have a somewhat more complicated tax return, you may want to buy a tax preparation software program such as TurboTax or TaxCut. Once you install the program (either one) you will be asked questions, such as "Did you have medical expenses this year?" As you go through answering the questions, the software will fill in your tax forms for you. The next thing you know, you'll have a completed tax return with the option to e-file or to print the return and file by mail.

I suggest using e-file only if you can send in for the rebate, so that it does not cost anything. Otherwise just print and send in the return by mail. If you e-file, and you are eligible for a refund, it will be deposited in your account in about 10 days. If you send your payment by mail, and request a direct deposit, it may take an additional five to seven business days. If you mail the payment and ask for a check to be sent, it could take about one full month before you get your refund. Most states also allow the state tax return to be electronically filed on the state website. You do not need any software; you can input the data directly onto the website.

If you are still uncomfortable, and you would prefer to have a professional look at your taxes, you have several options available. Whatever you decide, hiring a professional will be the most expensive option. Of course, if your preparer helps you find deductions or credits that you would have missed on your own, it may actually pay to hire a professional to do your taxes. You are probably wondering what type of professional you should use and how much you should pay.

First, let me tell you that the more work you do on your own, the more it will save you. Most professionals charge by the hour, which means if you have all of your receipts and paperwork organized and ready, you will save money. If your tax preparer has to call you up or have you come back to the office several times to deliver more tax relevant documents, you will be wasting your own time and your own money.

With that said, let's consider your options. If you have a relatively simple return then you could use a chain preparer such as H&R Block or you could use an independent tax preparer. If your return is more complicated, you could use a trusted independent preparer or an accountant. If it is really complicated, such as business income or difficult issues that deal with estate and inheritance taxes, then I would recommend an attorney, an accountant or an enrolled agent. An enrolled agent is certified by the IRS (by passing certain exams) and is allowed to represent you during an audit (not that you should need one).

Whatever you decide, there are a few things I need to warn you about. Many of the chain tax preparers will try to persuade you to take your refund with you the day they file your taxes, either by a refund anticipation loan, or some other "product." This really is a waste of money. After all, you will be getting your refund in about a week to 10 days if you file electronically and have your money direct deposited. You are basically paying them to let you borrow your own money for a few days... and you are paying them quite well. They try to feed on the fact that any money coming back to you is "unexpected" or "unbudgeted" income. They figure, and unfortunately they are right in many cases, that a person who is expecting a refund doesn't consider that the fees they paid cost anything because they are still getting money back. If you are due a $250 refund and they charge you $25 to pay you $225 right away, you may just be happy you got $225. Don't be "swindled" out of your other $25. Just thank them kindly and wait until the money shows up in your bank a few days later. Then buy yourself a steak dinner or something; it's your $25.

Also, avoid any type of loan where they pay your tax bill (assuming you owe), if at all possible. Keep in mind that you have until April 15th to pay the money owed, no matter when you file your return. If you are in bad financial shape, consider an offer in compromise. This is not for everybody, but there may be circumstances where you just can't come up with enough money to pay the taxes owed. Refer to IRS Form 656. Contact the IRS at 1-800-829-1040. Borrowing money to pay your taxes is just a double strike against your finances. Taxes are bad enough without paying extra fees or interest charges on top of what you already owe.

Tax Brackets

One of the only tax-related concepts that I find people misunderstand more than the tax returns themselves are the tax brackets. People usually don't understand how our progressive tax system works. I'll admit, it is quite confusing, at least in the beginning. To make things more complicated, the tax brackets change constantly based on new tax laws such as tax relief laws or tax increase laws (you can guess which one makes them go up and which one makes them go down).

So what is a progressive tax system? Basically, the more money you make, the more you pay. But wait, there's more. Not only do you pay more, you also pay a larger share of your income. As an example, if you make $1,000 and pay 10% you would pay $100 in taxes. If someone else made $10,000 and paid 10% they would pay $1,000. Both of you paid 10% in taxes, but the person who made more paid more. That is a flat-tax system. Now if the second person had to pay 20% because they made more money, they would pay $2,000 in taxes (20% x $10,000). You see, not only did they pay more ($2,000 compared to $100) but they also paid a larger share of their income (20% compared to just 10%). That is a simple example of the progressive tax system. As you'll see, it is slightly more complex than that.

An important point to remember is that different amounts of your income are taxed differently at each bracket. In other words, if you are in the 33% tax bracket it does not mean that you pay 33% taxes on all of your income. If you are in the 33% tax bracket, your *marginal tax rate* is 33%. You will pay 33% on each *additional* dollar you make. The first portion of your income was taxed at just 10%. Look at the example below, based on the 2010 tax rates for a single filer.

Tax Bracket	Taxable Income
10%	up to 8,375
15%	8,376 – 34,000
25%	34,001 – 82,400
28%	82,401 – 171,850
33%	171,851 – 373,650
35%	373,651 or more

For this example, we'll assume the taxpayer has $40,000 in taxable income. As you can see, this taxpayer would be in the 25% tax bracket. To calculate the tax liability, take the first $8,375 x 10% = $837.50. The next $25,625 x 15% = $3,843.75 and the last $6,000 x 25% = $1,500.00. So, this person's tax liability is $837.50 + $3,843.75 + $1,500.00 = $6,181.25.

As you can see, they are not paying 25% of all of their income, just the portion that is greater than $34,000. If they were to earn $1 more, they would pay 25 cents in tax on that dollar. If they were to get a $1 tax deduction, they would pay 25 cents less in taxes.

Of course, you also pay other taxes as well from your income. Most people pay a state tax. Also, we pay Social Security tax and Medicare tax. Your employer normally takes these "payroll" taxes directly out of your paycheck. Social Security and Medicare combine for 15.3%. However, your employer pays 7.65% and you pay 7.65%. Your employer may also take other non-tax payments out of your paycheck including your 401(k), health insurance, life insurance, etc.

Minimizing Taxes

Perhaps your biggest concern is minimizing your tax burden. The details of how the system works may not be as important as making sure you don't pay any more than you absolutely have to. In order to minimize what you pay in taxes, you have to first understand the three basic ways of paying less: credits, deductions, and deferrals.

You may recall from earlier in the chapter a tax credit is a dollar-for-dollar reduction in the amount of taxes you will have to pay. For instance, a $100 tax credit reduces your total tax contribution by $100. That's simple enough. A tax deduction reduces your total taxable income by the amount of the deduction. Another way to look at it is that a deduction reduces your tax contribution by the amount of your tax bracket. For example, if you are in the 25% tax bracket and you get a $100 deduction, you will save $25.00 ($100 x 25%) in taxes. As you can see, you want to make sure you claim all of the credits that you are eligible to take.

Chapter 14 Action Step

This is just a review. I want you to go back through the chapter and understand the difference between a tax deduction and a tax credit and how they affect the amount of tax you have to pay. If you want some extra credit, look for deductions or credits you have not used before, such as charitable contributions, student loan interest, or moving expenses. You will have to research these carefully (or use a tax preparer), but if you are entitled to them, then use them.

Chapter 14 Summary

❑ When first starting out, your taxes may be very simple. As you add mortgages and other deductions, they get more complicated.

❑ You are responsible for your tax information, even if your employer does not send your W-2.

❑ Credits directly reduce the amount of taxes you must pay, while deductions and deferrals reduce the amount of taxable income you owe, so you only save a percentage of these amounts.

❑ Do not pay an extra fee for your tax preparer to give you your refund immediately, since you will receive it in a matter of days with e-file.

Part V: Putting the "Personal" Back in Finances

"College will teach you how to 'do' something;
I want to teach you how to 'be' something"

15. Have it Your Way

➢ Know what *you* want out of life

➢ How to handle all of the pressure around you

➢ Live your life to its fullest

16. Just the Three of Us: How Money Affects Your Relationship

➢ Learn to talk about your money

➢ Be prepared, opposites do attract

➢ Use each of your strengths to maximize your finances

17. Ooh, Let Me See Your Ring!

➢ Prepare yourself for the wedding

➢ What to expect once you get married

➢ Be prepared for your first child

15
Have it Your Way

Sometimes when people talk about finances, they get too caught up in the numbers. I have a tendency to do the same, since I am a numbers person. After all, what can be more objective than a spreadsheet that calculates how much you need to save, or what percentage of your income you should be spending in each budget category? Left to our own device, we can justify just about anything ("I'll start saving next year," or "I'll charge it to the credit card since I have a low introductory rate."). That is why we need objective advice. But that is all it is, advice. In most cases we all need objective advice when dealing with our finances, but we are not objects. We are people and we need some subjective, personal direction as well.

Know What *You* Want Out of Life

I could tell you that you should save 10% of what you earn towards retirement, and I may be exactly right. But what I don't know, without asking you first, is what your retirement plans are. If you make $50,000 per year and you are 25 years old and you want to retire by age 45, then saving 10% of your income might not be enough. On the other hand, if you are 30 years old, have already saved $150,000, you are making $80,000 per year and you don't plan to retire until age 70, maybe you could actually save a little less in your retirement account and do something more with your current income. The point is you have to first decide what you want for your life.

That is why I emphasized the concept of planning earlier in this book. Once you have decided on a plan, only then can you decide how you want to reach it. There is nothing wrong with constantly revising your plan; as long as you know what your current starting point is when you do. This goes way beyond retirement. It covers all aspects of your finances such as how much of your income you should spend on your housing needs or whether it really is more important for you to purchase that new sports car now and defer some of your savings until later. I am not giving you the go-ahead to justify any and every decision; just make sure you know what the consequences of each decision are, and what your long and short-term goals are. This way you will be able to make the decisions that are in your best interest.

Along the way you are going to hear advice from many of the experts ('Pay off your highest interest rate loans first'), your family ('Buy the biggest house you can afford'), your friends ('I have this great stock tip that will beat the market') and of course sales people ('If you lease instead of purchase, you can get a better car for the same monthly payments'). What you have to be able to do is figure out when they are giving you sound advice, and when you need to tune them out.

Are you a low-risk or high-risk person? If you like to take risks, you will probably gravitate towards being a spender and borrowing for your current needs or putting your money into hot stocks or trying your hand at leveraged real estate. If you avoid risks at all costs you will probably shy away from borrowing, but will also keep your money in a local bank account that earns less interest than inflation.

Don't Get Scammed

People who are high–risk or desperate are much more likely to fall for get rich quick scams. Scams come in all shapes and sizes. If someone wants to give you money, but asks that you first give them money, you can pretty much bet it is a scam. If someone from Nigeria, or some other foreign country, wants to use your bank account to transfer millions of dollars, and give you a percentage, you are being scammed. If you are being guaranteed returns in double-digits (such as 10% or more), you are being scammed. Remember, if it sounds too good to be true, it is. People do not just give money away for nothing.

If you just send $5 to five people and each of them sends $5 to five people, what you will get is ripped off by $25 dollars and you will have committed mail fraud. In many sales organizations, one of your goals is to recruit other people so you can earn overrides on their commissions. Whenever the recruitment is where you make all of your money, and not on the sale of products, that is where you have a pyramid scheme, as opposed to legitimate multi-level marketing. If somebody on the Internet wants to show you how to become a millionaire with little or no effort by sending them $39.95, then what they mean by "show you how to become a millionaire" is, "you can watch as they become a millionaire" by ripping off people like you for just $39.95 at a time.

Here is a prime example of a pyramid scheme. You will get a letter or email from a lawyer or some other "trusted" professional so you know it is "real and legitimate". The letter will tell you to send money to a number of people, and those people will get a number of people to send money to you, and they get money sent to them, etc. Usually there will be some type of recruitment fee involved. If the recruitment fee involved is where your source of income comes from, and not from a legitimate product (such as cookware), you are probably getting scammed. Just because a friend is already hooked, doesn't make it any less illegal or less of a scam. In fact, in some scams, it is better for them to get friends and family to recruit each other because of the level of trust. Remember, don't let your emotions rip you off.

Who are You, Really?

You have to assess who you are in order to make the best decision according to your circumstances, and at the same time, understand that your personality may influence you strongly towards or away from risk. Once you understand your personality and how it relates to money, you will be better prepared to handle the one person most likely to talk you into spending large amounts of money irrationally throughout your life – You!

Don't Get Caught in the Trap!

Most people, when left to their own devices, just follow along with whatever society is telling them to do. After all, it's much easier to be a follower, right? As long as you are doing whatever everyone else is doing, nothing bad can happen. There is strength in numbers as the saying goes. Well, there is another saying also, "Misery loves company." Society would have you believe you should go ahead and buy, you can always pay later. But those same people will be right there harassing you for repayment when life turns ugly. What can happen to you though? You're young, you're smart, you have a college degree.

Another famous saying is, "Nothing is certain except death and taxes." One more thing is certain. Life. Life happens to everyone. For some people life happens when they are really young. For others it does not happen until they are really old. For the rest of us it happens right here in the middle. What do I mean by life happens? Businesses go bankrupt; unions become corrupt; employers move jobs overseas; spouses get sick; children sometimes come unexpectedly. And these are just some of the major examples. In our daily lives we have cars that blow head gaskets just a few months after we pay them off, dishwashers that leak all over the floor, pipes that burst, roofs that need to be replaced and other unexpected and unbudgeted events.

You may have heard of "Keeping up with the Joneses." A mentor of mine once said, "in our society, we spend money we don't have, to buy things we don't need, to impress people we don't know." He also said our neighbors "just live at a higher level of poverty." When your buddy gets a new sports car, or your neighbor adds a hot tub to their new deck, don't think that you need to buy those things just to keep up. Don't feel as though you are somehow not as successful just because you don't have as many play toys as those around you. For one thing, it is natural to only compare ourselves to those who have more, and never to those who have less.

It's also natural to accumulate jealousy from a number of different people. If the neighbor on the left gets a pool and the neighbor on the right gets a new car, we feel compelled to keep up with both neighbors, not just one. In some instances, the neighbors simply make a lot more money than you. Your goal is to simply spend less than you make, so maybe you can't afford what they can. It's certainly not worth risking your future retirement over a few nice things that will depreciate over time.

If buying more expensive "stuff" is important to you, then you need to look for ways to increase your income through career advancement, additional income sources, or starting your own business. However, before you begin those pursuits, please think about why it is you feel so compelled to have more stuff. A thriving business sector in our society is in mini storage units. Do you know why they are doing so well? Because we buy so much stuff we don't need and don't have room for, that we pay somebody to let us store the stuff we spent too much money on that we obviously don't need, otherwise we wouldn't be storing it in the first place. We are a consumer driven society. There is a lot of money out there, and you will make a lot of it in your lifetime. Other people want to get as much of your money as they can over the next 60+ years. At least now you know the rules of the game you are playing.

Money is a reflection of how we handle deeper issues in our lives. The way we handle money is simply an outward reflection on how we work internally. That is why insurance companies look at our credit history to determine what type of risk we are as a driver. A person who is generally disorganized, and does not care about their appearance, and does not respect their employer will be much more likely to have a low credit score than the type of person that cleans their dishes each night before going to bed, and always shows up to work on time and gives their best at the office.

You might think these two sets of traits are unrelated, but they can be used as indicators of one another. If your finances are in disarray, your life is probably in disarray also. I'm not talking about how much money you have. You can have millions of dollars and still be totally screwed up. Just look at Britney Spears. Her credit report might say she is okay because she has people that are paid to take care of her bills, but I'll guarantee you she loses more money each year through waste and fraud than many of us will earn over a lifetime.

When you start taking care of your life, your career, and your family, you will gradually begin to also take care of your finances. Paying your bills on time becomes more important, saving money for your future becomes essential, and putting money away for retirement becomes mandatory.

Live Your Life to its Fullest

For many of us our parents just went along with whatever society told them they should do. They had a thirty-year mortgage that lasted thirty years. They bought an expensive car and spent four or five years paying it off, so that they could get another expensive car and start over. They relied on their pension benefits from work or from social security for their retirement. They were really the first generation fully integrated into "buy now, pay later." For many of our parents they are still paying. They are still stretching out their mortgage. They are refinancing their credit cards into their mortgage, only to charge up their credit balances again.

Ask your parents how many times they bought things just to impress other people, and how many times they wish that they had not done so. What you will find is that you have the opportunity to make smart money choices earlier in your life than your parents ever did, because you are armed with the information that is hidden in our society.

Information that even some of the financial experts don't realize, or don't pay any attention to.

You now understand how debt works, how investing and savings work, and how financial products and services work. Add that to everything you learned already in order to get your degree and you are on your way. You will be watching your investments and savings grow over the next ten years. Soon you will be able to see your money work for you as you accumulate enough wealth and start earning more money from your investments than from your job. That's when you know you have finally made it. That is a real status symbol of success, not some fancy car that has to be leased because you can't really afford it in the first place.

You will be buying your cars with cash some day, and you will be able to buy a really nice car. And when you retire early, you can watch as your neighbors continue to work for many more years, all so they could borrow a newer car for a few years, or have the biggest house, or the nicest golf clubs or shoes and handbags whose names elicit curbside conversations in New York. I'm not saying don't have any fun with your money now. I'm saying don't have fun with tomorrow's money today, because tomorrow, you are going to wish it were still today.

Chapter 15 Action Step

Just for fun, I want you to go to the web and spend about 30 minutes researching common scams. Start with *www.scambusters.org* and try some government sites such as *www.sec.gov* & *www.ftc.gov*. Hopefully, by looking at some of the samples and telltale signs of fraud and scams ahead of time, you will be able to avoid getting scammed yourself.

Chapter 15 Summary

❏ Don't get too caught up in the numbers and percentages. They are only general guidelines. You have to apply your specific situation and needs to make the best decisions.

❏ Don't try to find the quick fix with money. Money and time go hand in hand, so if you are promised enormous amounts of money in a short period of time with no risk and no effort, run, don't walk, in the other direction.

❏ Don't get caught on life's treadmill method of finances where you always buy things one-step ahead of when you can afford it.

❏ Don't try to keep up with your neighbors. They may simply have more money than you or they may just be really bad at managing their personal finances and debt.

16

Just the Three of Us: How Money Affects Your Relationship

When do you start talking about money with the person you want to marry? Well, some guys try to bring up the topic ("Hey baby, check out my sports car") before their first date. Funny how that never really seems to work out. If you really want to crash a romantic evening, just start talking about money. Any topic will do -- how much you have, how much you don't have, how much the movies keep going up in price. Early in the relationship you really don't want to talk about money at all. However, once things get serious, it is actually one of the most important things to discuss, next to children.

Do you know what the number one cause of divorce is in this country? Well, yes, two married people not getting along. But what causes them to not get along? The number one reason is money! That's right, money is more a cause for divorce than sex or infidelity (cheating). Another terrible statistic is that almost half of all marriages end in divorce. That means most marriages probably have some sort of problem related to money.

The first thing you should do is figure out if you are a saver or a spender. The next thing to do is figure out if your spouse (or spouse to be) is a saver or a spender. Don't worry about who is what yet. This isn't like matching people according to what Chinese year they were born where a Saver should avoid the Spender and the Spender should avoid the Dragon. In many cases, opposites do attract. The good news is that it is okay to be different than your spouse. In fact, if you were both the same, there would be no point in having two of you.

Let me share a little story with you about balance. You see, my wife and I are a good balance for each other. She's not a big spender, but early in our marriage she would have spent a lot more if it weren't for my being the "checkbook police" as she put it. On the other hand, I would have been content living off of rice and water for two straight years so we would have been completely out of debt in no time (we had a lot of debt) and had established an emergency fund. Sure my way was more "mathematically" sound, but how boring is that? Who wants to spend the first two years of their marriage with no social outlet, no fun, and lousy food? That's what graduate school is for!

Sometimes both people in the relationship are spenders. This is bad for a while, but *almost* always, one of the two becomes a saver. The relationship and the spending cannot last if both partners spend without regard for their financial well-being. Don't always assume it is the husband that becomes the saver. In a little while we will talk about men and women and how they view finances.

It is also possible to have two savers in the relationship. Ironically, while this sounds good, this save-save thing can't last either unless they both get great pleasure from staring at their ever-increasing monthly account statements. If nothing else, the savers will begin to use their money for good causes. Some people don't see giving money to charity as spending, but the point is they are *using* their money. For the savers, they may have found a way to use it that is both responsible and fulfilling. In most scenarios, however, one spouse begins to realize they have all of this money and they want to begin using it. The other spouse may become so obsessed with getting to the next level, whether it's the next $1,000 or the next $100,000, they lose sight of the big picture. *Saving* to the point of destroying a marriage is just as bad as *spending* to the point of destroying a marriage.

Even if both of you are savers currently, you should talk about your goals. What will you do with your money? Is one person saving to reach a certain goal, only to spend more once that goal is reached? Just because you are both savers now does not mean you will both continue to be savers. It is important to agree on your goals now, so when you do reach that point, whatever it may be, you will not argue as much about what to do with your money. If one spouse says, "I thought we were saving this money so we can travel around the world," and the other spouse says, "I don't want to spend it now, we've worked too hard to save it," one of you could end up sleeping on the couch.

Learn to Talk About Your Money

Before you tie the knot, you should know a little bit about each other's money habits. You also need to be able to agree, or agree to compromise, on most of your goals. Just because you are dreaming of the white picket fence and the family car doesn't mean your spouse shares the same goals. Perhaps he or she prefers the idea of living in the city and renting an apartment or driving the newest sports car with all the accessories. The only way for your dreams to really become a reality is if you share them early on in your relationship and find some common ground.

You need to find out what each of you will be bringing to the table. If one spouse has $20,000 in debt while the other one has worked hard to save $20,000 in cash, the spouse who saved may feel resentment towards the one in debt. After all, no matter how you look at it, any money used to pay off debt once you are married is money that could have been used towards mutual goals instead, such as paying for your child's education, or making a down payment on a house. When you combine the net worth of the two individuals in this example it comes out to zero. That might be nice to the person who had the debt, but it wipes out everything the other spouse had worked so hard to save, up to that point in his or her life.

Once you learn what each person brings to the table, you will need to decide how to handle the debts and the savings. Decide now what percentage or dollar amount you want to try and save every month and how quickly you want to get out of debt. You should also decide how much you are willing to sacrifice to achieve those goals. Also, will you each contribute equally to the debt or will you have separate accounts and divide things up according to who brought in what debt, or who makes the most money, etc.

From what I have observed, if you want to destroy your marriage as soon as possible, then set up two separate accounts and keep everything separate. While I am sure there are some couples who do this and have a successful marriage (i.e. you do not get a divorce), you are more likely to struggle and have a business-like, or failed marriage. After all, separate just means you are not communicating about your finances.

Of course, before you are married, it makes sense to keep things separate. One way is to pay for things based on your salaries. For instance, if Bob makes $60,000 and Mary makes $40,000, then Bob pays for 60% of everything and Mary pays for 40%. This way they are each paying a proportional share of everything based on their income. If Bob thinks this is completely unfair, maybe Bob is not ready to be married yet and split things 50-50.

Call me a romantic, but I don't think a marriage should be run like a business. If a couple wants to have two separate accounts with each person being responsible for certain items (such as the mortgage or the car payment or the groceries), then I am not really sure why the two are married. They could have just been roommates. Sometimes, when a married couple starts to have problems, that's when they decide to start separating their accounts. That is the first step towards a divorce. May I suggest that you first seek counseling before going from a combined system to having two separate ones? It could save you in the long run.

With that said, I must add that there is nothing wrong with each person having their own spending account. In fact, I recommend that each person maintain a small amount of their own individuality through a discretionary account they can use on whatever they want, without having to answer to their spouse. In a sense, we are talking about an allowance. Each spouse would get an allowance of a certain amount of money every month. They can spend it all at once, or save it to buy something larger, such as an LCD television or a motorcycle. With the exception of certain costs such as transportation or lunches, both spouses should receive the same amount of allowance, even if one spouse does not work or one makes much more money than the other. After all, in most relationships one spouse works harder outside of the home, while the other one works harder in the home. Both are contributing to a successful marriage.

Be Prepared, Opposites do Attract

So what's the difference between how men and women spend their money? That is a tough question to answer since not everyone behaves the same way. We can make some generalizations about the two sexes and compare.

Most people like to get straight to the bottom line. Do men or women spend more? Different studies will give you different results, but it is safe to say that women generally spend more often, but it is a toss-up to decide who spends more money. What do I mean by women spend more often? Generally women shop more. They will buy that cute new "thing" that would look great on the mantle. Then they will purchase hand towels for the bathroom that can't be used, but are only for looks. They will also want that new blouse that looks great even though the whole reason they are at the store is to purchase planting soil for the flower garden. All said, we are looking at an extra $50 - $75 in this shopping trip. Multiply that by 52 weeks per year and you can see where your money goes.

What about the men? What do they do? Most men who are going to get potting soil, get potting soil. Thus, they spend $0 extra. But when that new drill set comes out for just $160, they need it. What about the 50-inch television set? There goes another $2,000. Of course we don't even need to talk about the sports car, pick-up truck or fishing boat purchases because we already see where this is going.

When men make a purchase, it is usually a large purchase. Women generally make many smaller purchases. Depending on the person and the relationship it may be very hard to determine off-hand who spends more, but keeping score makes your relationship seem more like a game. And with games, only one person can win, but both end up lonely.

The best way to battle the tug-of-war in your finances is to establish a realistic spending plan. Ideally, the two of you would each have an "allowance." Each person has their own set amount of money they can spend every month, without being held accountable to it by their partner (within reason). This is not the same thing as having two separate accounts. While everybody can name one couple that claims to successfully keep two separate accounts, it generally leads to divorce. It is very rare to find a successfully fulfilling marriage where the two partners have separate accounts.

It's hard to believe money could have such an effect on marriage, but it really is a major part of any relationship. Financial matters should not be taken lightly when you are combining two individual lives into one comingled relationship. The way the two of you handle money, as a couple, is a reflection on how you will handle the other aspects of your marriage. If someone is carefree and haphazard with their money even though they know their actions affect two people, you can be assured they will be haphazard about other aspects of the relationship (for example, they may forget to call you when they are going to be late for dinner). If someone hides certain money issues from their spouse or "cheats" by hiding income and spending on themselves, they may be inclined to cheat in other ways too. The list of similarities goes on, but I think you get the picture.

Ultimately, since you have two people in a relationship, you will have two personalities, and at times those personalities will conflict. What both of you have to keep in mind is that you are working as a team; you both have strengths and weaknesses, and you should work together to make the most of each. Nothing is more formidable than a strong marriage between two people who have learned to work together towards a common goal.

Use Each of Your Strengths to Maximize your Finances

Is your wife a whiz at math? Does your husband enjoy looking for coupons? Do you both enjoy yard sales? Find out what each of you enjoys, and what each of you can handle and divide the responsibilities accordingly. In my household, I take care of the finances (making sure the bills get paid, handling insurance and investments issues, etc.), while my wife usually takes care of the coupons and the pets (making appointments with the vet, etc.).

It does not really matter who does what in terms of taking care of the finances as long as neither one of you resents what the other is doing. If both spouses really want to handle all of the finances, or perhaps neither spouse does, then you can try doing them together. If you can make that work, you will truly be among a very rare and elite group of couples. Another approach is to rotate. Perhaps you could take turns every six months. Whatever approach you take to handling your money issues, be sure you are open with each other and you keep each other informed. In some marriages, especially those in the upper-middle to upper-income brackets, one spouse tends to hide money from the other. This is a dangerous habit to begin and it may be indicative of other trust issues within the marriage.

Remember, once you are married your money habits, including whether you pay your bills on time, affect two people (or more if you have children). You have to remember you are responsible for multiple people now. In fact, the money habits you bring into the marriage will affect both of you, especially if you have a bad credit history. It could affect whether or not you can get a car loan or a mortgage. Don't get too caught up in this issue. As long as you were upfront with your spouse from the beginning (as I mentioned at the beginning of the chapter), there will be no negative surprises.

Think Ahead

Let's assume a young married couple, we'll call them Bob and Sally, are each making $40,000 per year after just a few years into their marriage. They have a nice car, but not the SUV Sally wants or the cool sporty looking convertible for Bob. On top of that, they have extra money every month so they decide to go ahead and buy a home. Because of their income, they qualify for a bigger home than first imagined, and they are able to get all kinds of furniture on credit (after all, it's a new home so they need new furniture, right?).

Now, let's suppose Sally gets pregnant. Perhaps it was planned, or perhaps not. Either way, have they decided what they are going to do? What if six months into the pregnancy the doctor insists Sally must go on bed rest during the last trimester? What if Bob and Sally decide they really want one of them to stay home to raise their child, especially after realizing day care will cost them almost $12,000 per year. Maybe it is not even a money issue, but they simply want to raise their child and not use daycare. Either way do you see the problem? They are not in a position to go from $80,000 per year to $40,000.

The point here is that a young married couple should try to base their financial spending decisions on one income, especially once they decide to start a family. At the very least, before getting a mortgage, the couple must consider what they will do once their income is reduced. If Bob was making $60,000 and Sally was making $20,000 and she was going to stay home, the situation would not be as severe. In fact, Sally's salary is so close to the cost of daycare that it may not make much sense for her to continue working (as a financial decision) once the baby is born.

Ideally, after just a few years of marriage (or perhaps a few months in some cases), a couple could live off of one income while saving the second income towards an emergency fund, then a down payment for a home or a car, and then just to save. In the above scenario, if Bob and Sally saved half of their take-home pay, not only would they be able to easily adjust their spending to one income after the baby arrives, but they could have saved such a large amount of money towards their down payment that their monthly mortgage payment could be much lower. Plus, they would have some extra savings to get them through all the unexpected child expenses such as diapers, babysitters, etc.

Do not allow yourself to be cornered into making bad decisions for your family because of poor financial planning early in your marriage. While we may be living in a two-income world, it is possible to thrive on just one income if you plan right from the beginning and if you are willing to focus on your priorities and make some short-term sacrifices. Keep in mind with two incomes you are twice as likely to lose one of them at some point.

Your action step, if you are married or engaged to be married, is to create two budgets, one based on your combined salaries, the other based on a single salary. Look at what you would have to do if forced to live off of one income for a while (such as a job loss, etc.). Now, determine what your future plans are in terms of having children, caring for them, leaving the workplace, and returning to work (if desired) once your child starts school. Use these decisions to guide you as you make big financial decisions over the next couple of years. By planning ahead now, you could avoid possible future disasters, and you may be able to enjoy your pregnancy more if and when the time comes.

Chapter 16 Action Step

Your action step, if you are single, is to plan the next five years of your life, financially. Look at when you may be married, if and when you will have children, what type of home you will want, what your career will look like, etc. Create a plan now that incorporates your future goals. Perhaps it will indicate that you should save more now, reduce your expectations, or maybe just marry someone very wealthy (just joking). Take advantage of the fact that you have not yet put yourself into the financial corner that so many married couples find themselves.

If you are already married, then sit down with your spouse and discuss your next five years together. Talk about what you want, where you see yourself and each other in the next five years and what you want your money to go towards. Be prepared, this could be eye-opening.

Chapter 16 Summary

❑ You should learn to communicate with your spouse about money issues.

❑ Before you get married, you should know each other's financial situation, including debts, assets, and financial goals.

❑ Opposites can attract, so find out early if your spouse is a spender or a saver. Be honest about which of the two describes you.

❑ When you are married, all of the money belongs to both of you, no matter who earns more. Decide ahead of time how you will divide and use the money, or if it will be a 50-50 split.

17
Ooh, Let Me See Your Ring!

Marriage. I almost don't know what to tell you. (I know what I'm thinking, but my wife will probably read this…eventually). Admittedly, my wife did most of the work for our wedding. Sure I showed up and rented a tux, but she did most of the *real* work. (Men, these are the types of comments that will earn you points.)

Financially speaking, there are a lot of expenses that go into a wedding, even if your parents are paying for it or helping with the expenses. According to *www.SmartMoney.com* the average wedding today costs between $21,000 and $24,000, with 157 guests. That comes out to an average of more than $130 per person, so go ahead and register for those expensive gifts! The best advice I can give is to make sure this will be your one and only wedding.

First of all, who cares about the average wedding? You want yours to be better than average, right? Actually, you can have a beautiful wedding for much less than the average price. You just have to know what you are doing and where to shop.

Of course there are some wedding expenses that are not part of the more than $20,000 price tag. For instance, there is the engagement ring, and the bridesmaids' dresses, etc. Usually, the bridesmaids, groomsmen, and parents all pay for their own expenses. The engagement ring will be discussed later.

By reducing costs in the right areas, you can have a beautiful wedding well under $10,000. Look for ways to reduce your reception costs and you could be well on your way to saving a fortune. The largest single cost is the reception. You can also save money on the invitations. Shop around and find the one you want that fits within your budget. There's always going to be a better invitation if you just spend a little more… You could try to keep the rehearsal dinner from being too expensive by either going to a nice, yet reasonable restaurant, or by having it catered (perhaps in the church where you will be having your wedding). The photographer is somewhere you do not want to skimp. These are pictures of your wedding! However, you may want to consider having someone in your family video the wedding instead of paying a professional. Finally, the limousine is not really a wedding necessity. Sure it's nice, but maybe you can swing a favor, or just have a friend drive you to the reception (assuming this friend has a really cool car, or a convertible, etc.).

Here are a few more tips to help reduce the cost of the wedding:
> Buy a used veil, or borrow one from a friend or family member. It's the dress that really matters, not the veil.
> Purchase inexpensive white shoes, or ones that can be worn again. They will be more comfortable and nobody really sees your feet (this only applies to long dresses).
> Use single flowers in bud vases to decorate the tables. This is inexpensive, but gives the feel of flowers everywhere.
> Purchase your invitations online through one of the many companies mentioned in any one of the several hundred bridal magazines you now own.
> Have a buffet style dinner.
> Purchase a smaller fancy wedding cake, but order an additional sheet cake to be cut up and used for the guests.

Let's get back to the reception. There are really three ways to reduce the cost of the reception, (1) Invite fewer guests, (2) Find a place that charges less per person, or (3) Only invite one side of the family. Hopefully option #3 is not something you have considered, so let's stick with options #1 and #2. The earlier you plan for your wedding, the more options you will have.

If you are going to have the reception at a hotel or restaurant, shop around and compare menus and prices. Some places may charge a lower price if your reception begins or ends by a certain time. Try to select at least two entrees (chicken and lasagna for example) as well as some vegetables. (If I'm invited, I'll take the chicken.) If your budget permits, you may want to offer a cheese tray for the guests to eat while waiting for your arrival.

You may choose to have the reception at your home, your parents' home, somewhere outdoors, or at your church or community center. Assuming your family is not preparing the meal, you need to search for someone to cater your reception. Compare prices and menus just as you would with a hotel. Talk to friends and find out who they used, and if they would recommend their caterer. Sometimes the caterer may offer to let you sample their food which may prevent you from choosing food that will cause your guests to complain.

Food is a large part of the wedding. In fact, for some guests it pretty much defines the whole reception (guys). Normally you should order for at least 10% more people than the number of RSVPs. Some guests may take more food. Others may show up even though they did not RSVP, or they may bring an extra guest. On the other hand, you will have some guests who RSVP but don't make it to the reception. Still, it is better to have a little too much food than not enough.

Buying the Ring (A Guide for the Guys)

The engagement ring is normally purchased well in advance of a wedding. The average ring (sorry guys) costs around $3,000. Some in the diamond industry would have you believe you should spend two months' salary on a ring. Well, that just depends on how much you make. You can purchase a nice diamond (sorry ladies) for under $2,000. If you are on a tight budget (such as still in college) you could even go less than $1,000.

Keep in mind this ring is something she will probably wear for the rest of her life, so don't skimp. On the other hand, since life seems backwards, we tend to buy the ring during the poorest period of our lives (just after we get out of college, working an entry level position, and still paying off college loans). Of course the trend is that men are waiting a little longer to get married, so you may be able to afford more. Remember: don't destroy your finances just to buy a ring. It will be very difficult to start your marriage with such a large debt looming over your heads.

When shopping for a diamond, remember the four c's: cut, color, clarity, and carats.

The cut is perhaps one of the most important features of the diamond. If a diamond is cut too deep or too shallow, it doesn't reflect the light (it won't sparkle). You want to hold your diamond in a shadow and see if it still sparkles. Trust me, it's the radiance of the diamond that *keeps* the romance in the ring.

The color is also very important. If the diamond is practically yellow, you can get a real big one for a smaller price, but who wants a banana on their finger? You want to get as clear a diamond as possible. The clarity will also affect the sparkle, but most importantly, it will just look more elegant.

The clarity refers to imperfections or inclusions. The scale runs from VS1 to I3. VS1 stands for very small inclusions. The "1" just means it is the best VS rating. The I3 has the most inclusions visible to the naked eye. If you look at the diamond you'll see the cracks and other imperfections in the diamond.

The carat is the weight (don't ask why they use carats). A one-carat diamond is sort of the benchmark for money. For a man, buying a one-carat diamond is showing the world you can take care of your lady. For women, having a one-carat is just more diamond to show off. Plus it's a large reminder that she has a man in her life. You can go bigger, but realistically most people stay at or below one carat. Most women don't need a full carat. In fact, sometimes a ¾ carat or ½ carat will look much bigger on her hand than you may realize, depending on the size of her fingers.

There are a few other things to consider. The shape of the diamond is very important. Some women prefer round diamonds, others like marquee, some prefer princess cut, and so on. The type of ring is also very important. Does she prefer yellow gold? Perhaps white gold? Maybe platinum? There are also rings with diamonds (or diamond baguettes) on the sides. They look like a solitaire (or single diamond) but with a smaller diamond on each side. No matter what type of ring you choose, be sure to get a 6-prong setting. The more prongs holding the diamond, the safer it will be. You may actually want to take her ring shopping at some point. I would not, however, take her ring shopping until you are prepared to buy a ring (within 6-12 months). No girl wants to go ring shopping, and then have to wait three more years.

Since you are spending so much money on the ring, you should get it insured. Normally, expensive jewelry is not covered by your regular insurance (such as homeowners or renters). You can buy a separate policy for the ring, or sometimes get a rider on your homeowners or renters policy (a rider allows for items that are not normally covered). Either way, it is not very expensive. You can normally purchase this insurance from the same agent you use for car insurance.

When it comes to the proposal, only you know your girlfriend. However, most women like to be romanced. Remember, this is a story they will be telling their friends for a long time. Also, most women like to see the guy get down on one knee. It's just a tradition. I am not going to give you "romantic" ideas, but I will tell you a few things not to do.

1. **Do Not** forget to bring the ring
2. **Do Not** drop or lose the ring
3. **Do Not** forget your girlfriend's name

That's about it for the ring. All I can say now is good luck!

The Wedding Plans

We've talked about the costs involved, so let's talk about the work. Weddings are not easy, but they are not impossible either. If you have a budget and a timetable, the two of you can get this done. I won't lie though; you will experience a lot of stress during the process, especially as the wedding day approaches. Just remember that thousands of people get married every year.

The first thing you need to do (after the engagement) is set a date, or an approximate date. If the two of you are not ready to set a date yet, then don't. Once you are ready, set it, but make it somewhat flexible. If you pick an exact date six months in advance (such as June 5th), you may drive yourself crazy trying to book a reception hall or a caterer. Perhaps they have openings one or two weeks later (such as the 12th or 19th). The following are some other aspects of the wedding to consider:

- Number of guests
- Flowers
- Clergy
- Musician
- Photographer
- Videographer
- Band or D.J. for the reception
- Location of the rehearsal dinner
- Honeymoon
- Gift registration
- Invitations
- Caterer

I know for the men out there, we do not spend more than three or four minutes in our life even thinking about our wedding, and those minutes usually revolve around the honeymoon anyway. In order to be better prepared, I have included a 12-month checklist. If your wedding is in less than 12 months, you will have to speed things up accordingly. Remember, there is so much to do in order to get ready for a wedding, but don't get so caught up in the wedding that you forget about the marriage. Keep focused on each other for the next twelve months and everything will go a little smoother, at least tempers will not flair quite as much.

The 12-month Checklist for the Groom

12 months

- ❑ Buy the engagement ring
- ❑ Ask her to marry you! (I highly recommend asking her father first—It's traditional and it shows her family you respect them.)
- ❑ Estimate how much you will be able to spend on the wedding (another good reason to have asked her father for permission – he may be more inclined to help)
- ❑ Look into the availability of every person and place you need to reserve (Clergy, Church, Reception Hall, Florist, Photographer, Caterer, Musician, Band, etc.)
- ❑ Remind your fiancée that you love her

6 months

- ❑ Plan the honeymoon (make arrangements)
- ❑ Choose your best man and groomsmen
- ❑ Verify reservations (Clergy, Photographer, etc.)
- ❑ Remind your fiancée that you love her

4 months

- ❑ Choose your formalwear and make arrangements for the groomsmen, etc.
- ❑ Update your address list (hint: call your mother)
- ❑ Remind your fiancée that you love her

2 months

- ❑ Get your documents together (birth certificate, passport, etc.)
- ❑ Check on the requirements for a marriage license (blood tests, waiting period – probably not applicable in Las Vegas)
- ❑ Register for gifts
- ❑ Address and send the invitations, within the next two weeks
- ❑ Make wedding night reservations (secretly)

1 month
- ❑ Remind your fiancée that you love her

- ❑ Confirm menu decisions with the caterer
- ❑ Confirm details with the photographer
- ❑ Make sure your groomsmen have been fitted for their tuxedos
- ❑ Remind your fiancée that you love her

2 weeks
- ❑ Notify everyone of the rehearsal dinner details
- ❑ Get your hair cut. (It will still look good for the wedding, plus if they mess it up there will be just enough time for it to recover. Note: This is not the time to see what it would be like to shave your head.)
- ❑ Confirm transportation arrangements (limousine, friend, etc.)
- ❑ Get your marriage license!
- ❑ Remind your fiancée that you love her

1 week
- ❑ Pick up the wedding bands
- ❑ Pack for the honeymoon
- ❑ Get the cash together for the various fees (Clergy, Musician, etc.)
- ❑ Confirm everything (honeymoon, wedding night reservations, caterer, photographer, etc.)
- ❑ You may be safer avoiding your fiancée this week, but still make a point to remind her that you love her

2 days
- ❑ Get your tuxedo (or whatever you are wearing) and make sure your groomsmen have done the same
- ❑ At this point your fiancée won't really care if you love her or not – you're doing this thing no matter what – but you may want to drop a quick text message that you love her

1 day
- ❑ Attend the rehearsal dinner
- ❑ Give gifts to the groomsmen
- ❑ Give the rings to the best man (unless you want to wait until the wedding day)
- ❑ Confirm all the details with your best man
- ❑ Spend a few moments alone with your fiancé

❑ Breathe!

Wedding Day

❑ Have plenty of cash on hand (for tipping and the unexpected that may occur)
❑ Bring a *new* white handkerchief (for your wife, of course)
❑ Confirm your wedding night reservations
❑ Bring the marriage certificate!
❑ Compliment your fiancée on how beautiful she looks

After the Wedding

❑ Send thank you cards
❑ Enjoy your marriage
❑ Read this book again (but you can skip this chapter)!

The 12-month Checklist for the Bride

Before I begin, it goes without saying that you may want to look through the groom's checklist and verify that he is on task. Perhaps a better approach is to go through his best man and have him nag your fiancé.

12 months

❑ Estimate how much you will be able to spend
❑ Look into the availability of every person and place you need to reserve (Clergy, Church, Reception Hall, Florist, Photographer, Caterer, Musician, Band, etc.)
❑ Begin your guest list
❑ Remember, you are getting married because you are in love

6 months

❑ Make sure your fiancé is taking care of the honeymoon plans
❑ If necessary, get your passport (or update it)
❑ Choose your maid of honor and bridesmaids
❑ Announce your engagement in the newspaper(s)
❑ Select your gown and the dresses for the bridesmaids
❑ Put your deposit money on all the wedding services (photographer, etc.)
❑ Remember, you are getting married because you are in love

4 months

❑ Verify the gown and dresses are on their way

- ❑ Update your address list
- ❑ Order invitations
- ❑ Check on both mothers to see if their clothing has been ordered
- ❑ Remember, you are getting married because you are in love

2 months

- ❑ Register for gifts. Be sure that at least one of the stores you use is a national (or regional) chain if several of your guests will be coming from out of town
- ❑ Verify all of your important documents are together (passport, birth certificate, etc.)
- ❑ Address and send the invitations within the next two weeks
- ❑ Choose wedding rings
- ❑ Order the wedding cake
- ❑ Purchase gifts for the groom and your attendants
- ❑ Schedule any necessary appointments such as your hairstylist
- ❑ Remember, you are getting married because you are in love

1 month

- ❑ Finalize your menu
- ❑ Be sure everyone has been fitted for their wedding formalwear
- ❑ Attend all of your showers
- ❑ Finalize rehearsal dinner plans and notify the attendants of the date and time
- ❑ Get the necessary papers for change of address (if you will be moving) and name change documents (if necessary)
- ❑ Remember, you are getting married because you are in love

2 weeks

- ❑ Double-check the groom's checklist (to see if he is on task)
- ❑ Try on your wedding gown
- ❑ Confirm all the details with the musicians
- ❑ Prepare the wedding announcement(s) for the newspaper

- ❑ Make sure the marriage license is taken care of (or will be)
- ❑ Remember, you are getting married because you are in love

1 week

- ❑ Pay your next two or three weeks worth of bills
- ❑ Pick up the wedding rings
- ❑ Give the caterer the final count of guests from your RSVPs
- ❑ Pack for your honeymoon
- ❑ Re-confirm all the details with any reservations, appointments, etc.
- ❑ Remember, you are getting married because you are in love

2 days

- ❑ Make sure the marriage license is in your fiancé's possession
- ❑ Make sure your fiancé has his tuxedo
- ❑ Remember, your fiancé is just trying to stay out of your way at this point!

1 day

- ❑ Attend the rehearsal dinner
- ❑ Give your attendants their gifts
- ❑ Make sure everyone knows the start times and any other details (give copies of a schedule to the attendants if you want)
- ❑ Spend a few moments alone with your fiancé
- ❑ Do your nails (or have them done)
- ❑ Breathe!

Wedding Day

- ❑ Have your hair and makeup done
- ❑ Begin dressing about one and a half hours before the wedding (or earlier if having pictures taken beforehand)
- ❑ Bring the groom's ring

After the Wedding

- ❑ Send thank you cards
- ❑ Send your announcements and photos to the newspaper(s)
- ❑ Enjoy your marriage
- ❑ Read this book again (but you can skip this chapter)!

Splitting the Costs

You are probably wondering, "Who pays for what?" This is one of the most common questions before a wedding (The most common of course is, "Will you marry me?"). The list below should be used more as a guideline than a rule. Traditionally the bride's parents pay for the reception, while the groom's parents take care of the rehearsal dinner. With soaring wedding costs, couples marrying later in life, and other family situations, the rules have become more flexible. However, if you want to try to stick with tradition, the following is a good guideline.

Who Pays for What?

The Groom
- The engagement ring
- The bride's gift (yes you have to give her a wedding present)
- Corsages (for both mothers)
- Bride's bouquet
- Gifts for the attendants
- Fee for the clergy
- The honeymoon
- Accommodations for attendants who are coming in from out of town

The Bride
- The groom's gift
- Gifts for the bridesmaids
- Accommodations for attendants who are coming in from out of town
- Wedding gown

The Bride's Family
- Rental of the wedding site (i.e. church, mansion, etc.)
- Rental of the reception site
- Food/catering for the wedding reception
- Cake
- Flowers for decorations and the bridesmaids' bouquets
- Other decorations
- Wedding invitations, announcements, postage, etc.

- Gifts for the bride and groom (apparently paying for the wedding is not enough)
- Tips for servers
- Photographer
- Musicians
- Limo service
- Their own clothes

The Groom's Family
- The rehearsal dinner
- Gifts for the bride and groom (feel free to spend big!)
- Their own clothes

The Attendants (Male and Female)
- Their own wedding clothes (tuxedos and dresses)
- Gifts for the bride and groom

Remember, you do not want to start your marriage with conflicts among the family members over money issues. Long before the wedding, the family should agree who will pay for what. There may have to be compromises here. Do not try to play one side of the family off the other, and don't ask anyone to spend more than they can afford. Once it is decided who will pay for what it really should not be much of an issue. You should agree to listen to the input of both sides of the family, but still keep in mind that it is *your* wedding.

Since we are on the topic of paying for things, let's not forget to buy gifts for the attendants (best man, groomsmen, ushers, maid of honor, and bridesmaids). The cost of the gift depends on several factors, including how much you can reasonably afford. If possible, have the item engraved with the attendant's name. Here is a list of common gifts.

Gifts for the guys
- Money clip
- Pocket flask
- Pen set
- Mug
- Shot glasses
- Business card holder
- Fancy paper weight

Gifts for the ladies
- Jewelry to be worn during the wedding
- Anything from Pier One

I have a few suggestions that could make your wedding go by much smoother.
- ➢ Have a plate of food set aside for the bride and groom to be eaten after the ceremony. The couple will be starved and exhausted. There is just not enough time for them to eat as much as they need during the reception.
- ➢ Keep cash on hand, especially $5 bills and $1 bills for tipping. Also, have at least one $100 on hand if you can. It helps you feel more important and it is a good start to your honeymoon when you can pay for something with a $100 bill.
- ➢ Don't let anyone else know where you will be staying the night of the wedding (assuming you are not leaving for your honeymoon until at least one day later). Nothing good comes from other people knowing exactly where you will be spending your first night together.
- ➢ Have someone already selected to encourage visitors to sign your guest book. It's not fair to ask someone at the last minute.

Okay. Let's say there is no way you are ready to tie the knot just yet, but your best friend just asked you to be in his or her wedding. The groomsmen, bridesmaids, best man and maid of honor all have their own tasks to take care of. You don't want to let your friend down do you? Well, I've included a few checklists to help guide you through your responsibilities.

The Groomsmen
- ❑ Get fitted for your tuxedo
- ❑ Attend rehearsal dinner
- ❑ Provide transportation for bridesmaids if necessary
- ❑ Seat guests and pass out programs
- ❑ Unroll aisle carpet
- ❑ Make sure lighters are available for the candle lighting ceremony
- ❑ Dismiss guests by row at end of wedding
- ❑ Check the seats for personal items and remove the carpet, pew markers, etc.
- ❑ Stick around for the pictures

❑ Help in any other way if asked
❑ "Decorate" the groom's car (Note: If you use plastic wrap first, you will avoid damaging the paint)

The Bridesmaids
❑ Stay in constant contact with the bride-to-be to see if there are any errands that need to be run before the wedding
❑ Attend all of the pre-wedding showers and parties
❑ Be the bride's support group on her wedding day

The Best Man
❑ Do what you can to make it stress free (keep track of the check-lists)
❑ Take care of picking up the groom's formal wear and returning it after the wedding
❑ Arrange the bachelor party
❑ Make sure the groom looks his best (fix his tie, etc.)
❑ Hold the ring and the marriage license
❑ Give a toast at the reception
❑ Help take care of any other details as needed

The Maid (or Matron if you are married) of Honor
❑ Carry the check-lists and remind the bride of everything
❑ Stay near the bride and assist her as needed
❑ Make sure the bride's gown, etc. is perfect throughout the entire wedding
❑ Host a wedding shower (perhaps with her mother's help)
❑ Arrange the bachelorette party
❑ Make sure the bride does not leave any personal items at the church
❑ Help the bride get dressed
❑ Make the whole wedding go smoothly
❑ Give a toast at the reception
❑ Help in any other way the bride asks

Chapter 17 Action Step

If you are planning to get married, then set up a realistic budget with your fiancé. Write down the estimated expenses from each category (flowers, invitations, etc.) and make sure it is clear upfront who will be paying for what. Make sure both sides of the family agree on what their responsibilities are. If there are any misunderstandings or issues, you want to get them out of the way now, not three days before the wedding. If you are not getting married, then your action step is to share this book with (or buy a copy for) a friend who is getting married or graduating.

Chapter 17 Summary

- ❑ Weddings can be very expensive but there are plenty of ways to save on your costs without making the wedding appear cheap.

- ❑ When looking for an engagement ring, remember the four c's – color, cut, carat, and clarity.

- ❑ Men need to constantly remind their fiancée that they love them, especially as the wedding gets closer and the bride gets more stressed about all of the details of the wedding.

- ❑ Women need to remember the reason they are having the wedding in the first place is because they are in love and want to be married to their fiancé.

- ❑ Use the checklists to stay on top of everything to make sure your wedding day goes as smoothly as possible.

- ❑ Set aside a plate of food for the bride and groom for after the wedding reception. They will be starved and exhausted after their stressful day and they will not have had much time to eat during the reception.

- ❑ Have a happy and healthy marriage!

Appendices

Appendix A
List of Professional Job Sites

Note: Many job sites give you the ability to register your profile and search for jobs based on your criteria, and will then notify you by email anytime a job matches your search criteria. This is a useful tool since you will not have to log onto the site everyday to see if a new job has posted.

General
www.careerbuilder.com
www.collegegrad.com
www.collegerecruiter.com
www.hotjobs.com
www.monster.com
www.truecareers.com

Architects – The American Institute of Architects
www.aia.org

Business – Accounting, marketing, etc.
www.accounting.com
www.bankjobs.com
www.hrjobs.com
www.marketingjobs.com

Communications
www.journalismjobs.com

Education
www.academic360.com
www.higheredjobs.com

Engineering
www.engcen.com

Government - Federal government
www.usajobs.gov

Healthcare
www.globalhealth.org

Law
www.lp.findlaw.com

Non-profit
www.nonprofitcareer.com

Science
www.newscientistjobs.com

Technology
www.computerwork.com

Appendix B
Recommended Books

Extra Credit: The 7 Things Every College Student Needs to Know About Credit, Debt & Ca$h – by Bill Pratt, MBA

The Millionaire Next Door - by Thomas J. Stanley and William D. Danko

Financial Peace: Restoring Financial Hope to You and Your Family - by Dave Ramsey

How to Have More than Enough: A Step-by-Step Guide to Creating Abundance - by Dave Ramsey

The Automatic Millionaire: A Powerful One-Step Plan to Live and Finish Rich - by David Bach

The World's Easiest Pocket Guide to Renting Your First Apartment (World's Easiest Guides) - by Larry Burkett and Ed Strauss

Mortgages For Dummies, 3rd Edition - by Eric Tyson and Ray Brown

Home Buying For Dummies, 3rd edition - by Eric Tyson and Ray Brown

Insurance for Dummies - by Jack Hungelmann

Knock 'em Dead 2009: The Ultimate Job Search Guide (Knock 'em Dead) - by Martin Yate

Knock 'em Dead Resumes - by Martin Yate

Knock 'em Dead Cover Letters - by Martin Yate

Great Answers to Tough Interview Questions, 7th Edition - by Martin Yate

Appendix C
Recommended Websites

www.ExtraCreditBook.com
The flagship site for all of my articles and calculators. My blog and message boards are coming soon. You can also sign up for Extra Credit Tips, a monthly e-newsletter with tips on credit and debt and Money 101 – a free 30 day online money course. Feel free to download the Excel financial calculators as well.

www.TheGraduatesGuide.com
The site for this book. Free articles and downloads and other current information that affects college graduates and others age 18-35.

www.DaveRamsey.com
Dave is the country's premier expert on financial advice and getting out of debt.

www.nslds.ed.gov
This is the place to go to find lots of information about your student loans.

www.YoungMoney.com
The website for Young Money magazine. The site is designed for young adults, 18-35 years old. There are tons of articles from entrepreneurship to credit, and more.

www.SmartMoney.com
Smart Money is witty, to the point, and informative. One of the best personal finance sites that I have used, although their pages are a bit cluttered.

www.about.com
About.com has a host of informational sites on everything from weddings to investing.

www.BankRate.com
Bankrate.com houses articles and several useful calculators.

www.mycalculators.com
As the name states, this site houses several useful financial calculators (although they are not mine).

www.citibank.com
Check out Citibank's site and select Planning. Here you will find articles and calculators.

www.nolo.com
Contains several articles relating to tenants' rights.

www.rentlaw.com
A great resource for rental laws in all 50 states.

www.rent.com
Rent.com allows you to search most major cities for an apartment. It also has resources for getting a roommate.

www.edmunds.com
Edmunds is a must-use website for anyone about to buy or sell a car.

www.kbb.com
Kelley Blue Book is the most used reference to determine the value of a car.

www.hoovers.com
You can get some basic information about many companies here (such as number of employees, size of operations, etc.)

www.livecareer.com
A pioneer in free online career tests, helping people get and keep their dream careers. Their career center offers career advice, information about new careers, pay scale and average salary information, and a free salary survey report that covers most industries and job types.

www.careerpath.com
CareerPath.com by CareerBuilder.com is a career resource center that will assist you in making the right career decisions. Assistance is provided with career tests, advice and resources.

www.flexadministrators.com
Private website run by a company that administers flexible spending accounts for businesses. Their site includes useful information about flexible spending accounts including spending limits, etc.

www.irs.gov
Tax forms, instructions, etc. can all be downloaded from the official IRS site.

www.ScamBusters.org
Provides up to date information on Internet Scams, Identity Theft, and Urban Legends. If you are concerned about a possible scam or you want to know if something is real or just an Urban Legend, then visit this site.

www.sec.gov
If you are interested in investing and want to know about some of the technical stuff the government regulates, etc. then this is your place.

www.ftc.gov
The FTC includes the Bureau of Consumer Protection. They offer tips on how to avoid the latest scams, telephone fraud, etc.

Appendix D
Answers to Interview Questions

➢ *Where do you see yourself in five years?*
I see myself as an integral part of the team here. While I will have a small learning curve coming on board initially, within five years I will definitely be considered a significant and integral contributor to your organization.

➢ *Do you have any difficulty working with others?*
I have always enjoyed working with others. While I am certainly able to produce independently, as demonstrated by my achievements [mention an example with an organization or an academic achievement], I also love working with teams. I find that having more than one individual contributing to a project results in broader perspectives and builds relationships for future endeavors at the office.

➢ *Why do you want to work here?*
[This is where your research comes in handy]
My research on this organization shows that you offer room for me to contribute to your success while at the same time, I will be able to further develop my skills and expertise. It's a win-win.

➢ *Why should we hire you?*
My academic background is indicative of my ability to take difficult material and successfully understand it and apply it. In addition, I have experience outside of my education as I served on [list any organizations] and with my part-time job and my internship experience. As you can see, not only have I proven the ability to adjust to the working world, but I have a proven track record of success, already in my early career. What that means to your organization is that you are getting the benefit of hiring me at an entry level, without the usual risks involved with an untested candidate.

➢ *How well do you handle stress?*
I have learned quickly to adapt to stressful situations and manage them appropriately. Since stress is a regular part of our lives, I think the key is to recognize that and manage it. Since a lot of stress is

self-induced I have been able to "step out" of situations and look at them objectively. By planning properly and being organized, much stress can be avoided. For the stress that cannot be avoided, I break the situation down into manageable pieces, seek assistance where appropriate, and try to work logically instead of emotionally until the project is completed.

➤ *What are your strengths?*
One of my greatest strengths is my ability to improve efficiency. [Notice the use of actual situations] For instance, when I was in the Student Government I noticed that the process for requesting activity funds was cumbersome and confusing. I created an automated form and created and conducted a workshop for student organizations to take the mystery out of funding requests. Another example is...

➤ *What are your weaknesses?*
[Give a real weakness that is not detrimental to the job description, but show how you are working to improve]
I would say my greatest weakness is that I try to take on too much when I am the lead on a team project instead of delegating more. For instance [describe a situation]. What I have been doing to improve this weakness is break assignments down and work with group members to match their strengths with the individual tasks.

➤ *What is your biggest pet peeve?*
[Avoid anything offensive such as a particular style of music, religion, political party, etc.]
My biggest pet peeve is when individual group members do not pull their weight and just expect everyone else to pick up the slack. That is why when I am on a team, I try to break assignments down... [Show that you can resolve an issue, not just complain about it]

➤ *What do you think of your previous employer?*
[Never say anything directly negative]
My previous employer was kind enough to bring me on board and gave me the opportunity to really grow and develop my skills. Unfortunately, there was no opportunity for me to really develop into a position using what I learned from my college major, which is one reason I am looking forward to working with your company.

➤ *What did you like most about your last job?*
[Do not pick something that is completely the opposite of what your current job entails. For instance, don't talk about a 10 AM start time if you are expected to arrive at 8 AM every morning at this job]
I really liked the opportunity to work with a diverse group of people…

➤ *What did you like least about your last job?*
[Again, be careful not to be too negative]
While I loved many aspects of my previous position, there was simply no room for me to really use my skills and talents given the limited nature of the available positions.

➤ *What was the last book you read? What did you learn?*
[Needs to be appropriate and thought-provoking. The key is that you should read a book on occasion. You had to have at least read something in college for a literature class]

➤ *What starting salary do you expect?*
[Try to avoid giving a specific number. Too low and you sell yourself short. Too high and you may price yourself out of the position]
I realize that this is an entry level position. Of course, I also believe that I will bring a lot of value to your organization as well, given my background/education, etc. I am sure that once I understand exactly what this position will entail and once we both agree that I am the right person for the job, we will have no issue settling on a fair salary.

➤ *Do you prefer to work independently or with others?*
In my experience there is never an absolute. As part of an organization you are part of a team in some way, and as a team member there will always be aspects of any project that require individual work. With that said, I am flexible and I enjoy having some of each. Individual tasks allow me to really show my skills as I thrive on the independence, while working with others gives me the greatest chance to grow through the input and feedback of others.

➢ *Where else have you applied?*
[Unless there is some issue with telling them, just let them know. If you want to remain vague you can do that as well, per the example]
I have applied to a few other companies. I decided to only look at companies, such as yours, that are the top in their industry.

➢ *Why did you leave your last job?*
[This does not apply if this will be your first job. Otherwise stick with something related to lack of opportunity for you to develop, declining industry, etc. Nothing personal or directly negative relating to your previous employer]

➢ *Why did you choose your major?*
[I assume you have a good reason such as a certain person who inspired you or a situation that inspired you. You want to have a reason you chose your major. If it sounds like you just "happened upon it" it shows a lack of enthusiasm or drive behind your motivation and it may cost you the position.]

➢ *How do your experience and education relate to this job?*
[You may have to use your imagination. For experience, think back to the resume chapter. Customer service or sales can be applicable to any position, as can being detail oriented, etc. Connect the broad qualifications for the job with what you have done. If your major is not directly aligned with the position, think about how it can relate. For instance a math major can do reporting or programming if he or she focuses on the logic involved or the ability to analyze a problem and find a solution]

➢ *Describe a situation where you had to deal with a difficult customer.*
[More and more questions are looking for actual situations. Make sure you give an example with a positive result. Describe the situation, what action you took, and the positive result]
Once, I had a customer who was very upset that we did not stock the replacement part he needed. I took the time to look up the manufacturer's number, contact their parts department and find out how the part could be ordered. By the time we were done, the customer was able to order the part from the manufacturer, was very grateful for my assistance, and apologized for yelling at me.

➢ *Give me an example where you tried something new and it worked.*

When I was in Student Government I took an antiquated, confusing process and automated it. I knew it was different than what had ever been tried before at the office, but I was able to identify the pain involved from the customer's point of view. I created the automated fill-in form and held a workshop for organizations that wanted to request funding. The result [This is key] was that several organizations thanked me for the easy form, and several new organizations that had never requested funds before were surprised and grateful to find out there were funds available. The program resulted in saving the customer time, making the process easier, and resulted in several new customers.

➢ *Give me an example where you tried something new and it failed.*
[Use an example of a failure that you were able to use as a learning experience, and how you are now better because of it]

When I was in Student Government I took an antiquated, confusing process and tried to automate it. Instead of using a paper process, I created it in Excel with drop-down boxes, etc. to make the process easier. I also held a workshop to explain the new process to groups on campus. Unfortunately, the new form was not well received. Students were not accustomed to using Excel forms and I did not build enough checks into it to prevent others from messing up the formulas. Plus very few people showed up to my workshop. [What you learned] Because of that experience, I now realize it may be better to work with the customer during any new development so I can get their feedback before the project is complete. I also learned to better document instructions and to build more checks and balances so users of all levels can take something unfamiliar and successfully use it the first time. I also learned the importance of marketing and working with influential individuals in order to spread the word so that more people will come to workshops.

Appendix E
Additional Resources

The Major Credit Bureaus:

Experian
NCAC
P.O. Box 9556
Allen, TX 75013
1-888-397-3742
www.experian.com

Equifax
P.O. BOX 740256
Atlanta, GA 30374
1-800-797-6801
www.equifax.com

TransUnion
Customer Disclosure Center
Trans Union Consumer Relations
P.O. Box 2000
Chester, PA 19022-2000
1-800-888-4213
www.transunion.com

Sources

Chapter 1 – Statistic: More than two million college graduates. Source: National Center for Education Statistics: Projections of Education Statistics to 2017. Table 27 and Table 28.

Chapter 5 – Statistic: The average college graduate overestimates their starting salary by 44%. Source: Big Loans, Bigger Problems: A Report on the Sticker Shock of Student Loans, March 2001 (Tracey King and Ivan Frishberg); www.pirg.org.

Figure 5-2, Bi-weekly payroll withholding: www.irs.gov.

Chapter 7 – Various common tenant rights: www.rentlaw.com

Chapter 11 – Types of repayment options: Inceptia.

Types of repayment options: http://loanconsolidation.ed.gov/help/faq.html#option

Figure 11-1, Repayment options chart: Student Aid on the Web (www.studentaid.ed.gov) online calculators and Finaid.org online calculator (www.finaid.org).

Loan forgiveness: www.studentaid.ed.gov

Figure 11-2, Repayment periods:
http://loanconsolidation.ed.gov/examples/repyperiod.html

Loan consolidation:
http://studentaid.ed.gov/PORTALSWebApp/students/english/consolidation.jsp?tab=repaying
http://loanconsolidation.ed.gov/borrower/bconsol.html

Deferments:
http://studentaid.ed.gov/PORTALSWebApp/students/english/difficulty.jsp
http://studentaid.ed.gov/students/publications/student_guide/2009-2010/english/postponeloanpayment.htm#loandefermentsummchart

Income Based Repayment Calculation:
The Income-Based Repayment has many variables. You will have to use the online calculator and enter your information for a more accurate estimate. For this example the following variables were used, based on the default settings of the finaid.org income-based repayment calculator: Table Year = 2009, Family Size = 1, Discount Rate = 5.8%, CPI = 3%, State of Residence = Continental U.S., Income Growth Rate = 4%, Poverty Level Change Rate = 3%. In addition the following variables were used for this example: Loan Forgiveness = 25 years, Tax Filing Status = Single, Adjusted Gross Income = $30,000, First Loan = $35,000, Interest Rate = 6.8%, Minimum Payment = $10.00, Interest Rate Reduction = 0%. In this example payments begin at $172 per month and increase each year until year 19 when the payment reaches $403

per month and remains constant for the remaining three years (except the final payment which is $313).

Chapter 13 – Types of homeowner policies: http://www.insurance-education-group.com/home-policy-forms.html. Accessed: January 2, 2011.

80% rule: http://www.homeinsurance.org/articles/eighty-percent-rule-means-collecting-insurance-company.html

Chapter 14 – 2010 federal tax rates: http://www.taxfoundation.org/publications/show/151.html

Chapter 17 – Statistic: The average wedding costs between $21,000 and $24,000, with 157 guests. Source: SmartMoney.com Article: They'll Never Know: Eight Hidden Ways to Cut Wedding Costs. Updated on June 11, 2008.

Glossary

401(k): Retirement plan that allows workers to save a portion of their income while deferring taxes on the income saved and the earnings until withdrawal.

403(b): Retirement plan, specifically for public education institutions, non-profit organizations and self-employed ministers, that allows workers to save a portion of their income while deferring taxes on the income saved and the earnings until withdrawal.

Adjustable rate mortgage (ARM): A mortgage with an interest rate that periodically adjusts based on various financial indices.

Adjusted gross income (AGI): Used to calculate income taxes. Total Income, minus certain deductions, such as 401(k) or IRA contributions.

Automated Teller Machine (ATM): A standalone unit that allows financial institution customers to access their accounts, including withdraws of cash, without the need for a human teller.

Average daily balance: The total balance at the end of each day during a period divided by the number of days in the period (usually one month).

Back-load fund: A mutual fund with a commission representing a percentage of the selling price of the fund, paid at the end when the fund is sold.

Bank: A financial institution which borrows and lends money and acts as a pay agent for its customers.

Benefit period: The amount of time that a disability insurance will continue to pay benefits before it runs out or stops.

Bounced check: When a check cannot be honored by the bank due to insufficient funds. In other words, there is less money in the account than the amount of the check.

Capitalized interest (Student loans): On a student loan, accrued, unpaid interest can be added to the principal balance in certain circumstances. This is called capitalization.

Certificate of Deposit (CD): A form of savings where the funds must remain there for a specified amount of time before you can withdraw them (time deposit). If you withdraw the funds early you will pay a penalty and will likely lose money.

Checking account: An account held at a financial institution that allows you to write checks and make other regular withdrawals and deposits, normally used for everyday transactions.

Closing costs: The costs associated with purchasing a home in addition to the actual cost of the home, payable upon the transfer of ownership.

Compound interest: Interest that is allowed to earn interest that is added to the principal and so on.

Credit Union: A cooperative financial institution that is owned and controlled by its members. Similar to a bank in its purpose to lend and borrow money, but usually at rates more favorable to its members.

Credit (Tax): A tax credit actually reduces your tax liability dollar for dollar.

Debt: Owing money to somebody else for products or services provided that you did not yet pay for, whether you have to pay it right away or wait until later and whether you are being charged interest or not.

Deductible: The amount you must pay out of pocket before your insurance benefits will begin.

Deductions (Paycheck): The items that reduce your take-home or net pay such as insurance, taxes, etc.

Deductions (Tax): The items that reduce your taxable income as they are deducted from your Gross Annual Income, such as mortgage interest, dependents, etc.

Default (Student loans): On a student loan, if you fail to make a payment for 270 days or more, your loan is considered to be in default.

Deferment (Student loans): A period of time when your servicer will allow you to stop making payments. You may be granted a deferment for various reasons, including unemployment, economic hardship, and military service.

Deferral (Tax): Offsets on current taxable income. Taxes on the deferred income is paid later, such as when withdrawn from a retirement account.

Direct deposit: The electronic deposit of your paycheck directly to your bank account, eliminating the need to "cash your check" at a bank. Most companies either allow or require direct deposit.

Direct loans (Student loans): Low-interest loans for students and parents to pay for the cost of a student's college education. The lender is the U.S. Department of Education (the Department) rather than a bank or other financial institution.

Disability insurance: A form of insurance that pays a portion of the beneficiary's income in the event that the beneficiary cannot work or cannot work at the same level as before the onset of the disability.

Dollar cost averaging: Systematically investing a set dollar amount on a regular basis, without regard to the current or short-term financial market conditions.

Elimination period: The period of time after a qualified disability is determined to have begun and the time a disability insurance policy will make the first benefit payment.

Emergency fund: Money saved to cover unexpected personal expenses, such as replacing an appliance or fixing a car. Emergency funds protect consumers from debt.

Escalation clause: A clause on an offer to buy a house that specifies the prospective buyer will increase their offer by a set dollar amount above the next highest bidder, up to a limit.

Employee Stock Ownership Plan (ESOP): An optional plan that may be offered by a corporation, giving their employees the ability to purchase shares at a set price or the employers may choose to contribute to an employee's ESOP as part of a bonus or other means of compensation.

Eviction: The legal removal of a tenant from a rental property by a landlord.

Exemptions (Tax): A portion of income or revenue that is exempt from being taxed. The result is lower taxes.

Federal tax: This tax is deducted directly from your paycheck based on income tax brackets established by federal law.

Federal Family Education Loans (FFELP): A public-private partnership in which private, nonprofit and state-based lenders make federally guaranteed loans to students and parents. FFELP does not require collateral to get student loans at low interest rates. Some FFELP loans, like those made to parents, require a good credit history or a cosigner. FFELP was replaced by the Direct Loan Program as of July 1, 2010.

Federal Income Contribution Act (FICA): Also called Social Security, this represents 6.20% of your income that is deducted from your paycheck. Your employer also pays an additional 6.20%. Self-employed individuals pay the full 12.40%.

Federal student loan: A loan made by the federal government to pay for educational expenses. Before July 1, 2010, federal student loans were also made by private lending organizations, such as banks and financial institutions.

Fixed rate mortgage: A mortgage type that has a fixed or unchanging interest rate throughout the entire length of the loan.

Forbearance (Student loans): A period of time when you temporarily do not have to make payments on your loan, or your payment amount may be reduced. Interest accrues during a forbearance even if you have subsidized loans.

Foreclosure: The legal process in which a lender repossesses real property from a borrower after the borrower fails to make the necessary payments for a specified period of time. The lender may choose to sell the property, keeping the profits.

Form 1099: An information return for the U.S. tax system, usually provided to independent (non-employee) contractors to report income other than wages, tips, etc. (which are reported on Form W-2).

Front-load fund: A mutual fund with a commission representing a percentage of the purchase price of the fund, paid up front.

Flexible Spending Account (FSA): A tax-advantaged financial account that allows an employee to set aside a portion of his or her earnings to pay for qualified expenses. The money designated into the FSA is not subject to payroll tax. The two major FSAs are the Medical FSA (designed for qualified medical expenses) and the Dependent Care FSA (designed for qualified child care or adult care expenses).

Grace period: On a federal student loan, this is usually a six-month or nine-month period after you leave school or drop below half-time enrollment when you don't have to make payments.

Graduated payments: For student loans, payments that start lower than traditional payments and periodically increase until the final payments are higher than the traditional payments to compensate for the earlier, lower payments. Allows recent graduates to pay less while starting out and pay more as their income (theoretically) increases.

Gross pay: The total amount of income earned, before any deductions. The larger amount on a paycheck (Net Pay is the smaller amount).

Growth fund: A mutual fund that invests in growth stocks, or companies that are expected to have high earnings or revenue growth as opposed to larger, stable companies that pay dividends. Growth funds are very volatile.

Health insurance: Provides coverage for medicine, doctor office visits, hospital stays, and other medical expenses.

Hybrid mortgage: A mortgage type that combines a fixed rate period, such as 7-years, and an adjustable rate period for the remaining portion of the loan.

Identity theft: Through criminal means, capturing personal and financial information and using it for illegal purposes. It may include borrowing money in another person's name or withdrawing funds from the bank account of another without their knowledge or permission.

Index fund: A mutual fund that is passively managed and tries to mirror the performance of a specific index, such as the S&P 500. Expenses tend to be very low.

Institutional loan (Student loans): An institutional loan is a student loan made to a college student by the educational institution the student attends. The availability and requirements for the loans vary by institution.

Interest rate: A rate charged or paid for money that is borrowed or loaned. The rate is expressed as a percentage of the principal based on a period of time, normally annually.

Internship: A paid or unpaid temporary position emphasizing learning about the position. Usually designed for students, internships provide the opportunity to gain work experience in a specific field, and may allow the student to earn college credit.

Individual Retirement Account (IRA): A tax-deferred retirement account for individuals. A certain amount of money can be set aside annually, while the earnings are tax-deferred until withdrawn.

Junk bond: High risk bond with low credit ratings, which may result in significant or total loss or significant gains.

Lien: A legal claim against a piece of property that must be paid when the property is sold.

Lease: An agreement to use property for a specified period of time; includes automobiles as well as buildings such as apartments, homes, and business offices.

Life insurance: Pays an amount to the beneficiary upon the death of the insured person.

Life-changing event: A change in life-status (such as marriage, divorce, adoption, etc.) that allows you to change your insurance type selection through most employers (such as adding or removing coverage).

Load funds: A mutual fund that charges a sales or purchase commission, usually as a percentage of the amount invested or sold.

Loan balance: The amount of debt outstanding, or not yet paid on a loan.

Low-load fund: A mutual fund that charges a very small percentage front-load or back-load commission.

Market value: The price as determined by the current buyers in the market for the particular item.

Medicare: Represents 1.45% of your income that is deducted from your paycheck and used to fund the government run Medicare system. Your employer also pays an additional 1.45%. Self-employed individuals pay the full 2.90%.

Minimum balance: The lowest amount of money that you are permitted to have in an account at a financial institution without incurring fees.

Mortgage: A security for the loan that a lender makes to a borrower. It is normally based on the loan to finance the purchase of real estate.

Mutual fund: A professionally managed fund that pools money from many investors and invests that money in a group of assets, based on a stated set of objectives.

Net pay: The amount remaining in your paycheck after deductions are taken from your gross pay.

Network: Developing a social circle for the purposes of meeting people that can lead to mutually moving your careers forward.

No-load funds: A mutual fund with no commission; recommended for the average investor.

National Student Loan Data System (NSLDS): A website managed by the federal government where federal student loan borrowers can find information about their loans. Private loans and institutional loans are not listed in NSLDS.

Options trading: A form of stock trading that allows for extreme leverage resulting in the possibility of very large gains or very large losses. Each option usually represents 100 underlying shares, thus creating the leverage. Recommended for experienced traders only.

Perkins Loan (Student loans): A type of federal loan made by the educational institution that you attend. The availability and amount of the loan is determined by your financial need and the institution. The institution may hire a servicer to interact with borrowers, manage the loan records, and collect payments.

Placement agency: Matches job seekers with employers to place them in long-term, permanent positions.

Planned community: A community that typically has preselected builders with specific home models available. Sometimes amenities such as a clubhouse or community swimming pool may be part of the community.

Pre-approved mortgage: A lender determines the amount a borrower will be permitted to borrow for a mortgage based on verification of credit history, bank references, and employment. Final approval is subject to the determined value of the property.

Pre-qualified mortgage: A lender determines the amount a borrower will be permitted to borrow for a mortgage based on opinion, before verification. Final approval is based on verification of the borrower's financial information and the determined value of the property.

Principal: The amount owed on a debt or the amount of an investment. Interest is calculated on the principal.

Private student loan: A loan made by a lending institution such as a bank or other lender, for college education expenses. These loans often require credit checks and cosigners and have variable interest rates. The amount and terms of the loan are determined by the lender.

Renters insurance: Protects the renter's personal property (such as furniture within your apartment) and provides some liability protection as well.

Replacement value: The amount the insurance company will pay to replace your item at its pre-loss value, not the current market value which is lower due to depreciation.

Risk tolerance: The amount of uncertainty an investor is willing to tolerate for the purpose of increasing their investment gains.

Rollover IRA: Moving money from one eligible retirement account such as a 401(k) or other IRA to another eligible IRA. Commonly used when changing jobs.

Rule of 72: States that to estimate how many years it takes to double your savings or investments, divide 72 by the interest rate. Used for one-time investments or lump sum.

Savings & Loan: A financial institution that generally accepts savings deposits and makes mortgage loans.

Savings account: A bank account that pays interest and is not meant to be used for daily withdrawal transactions.

Security deposit: An amount of money usually required by landlords before you can rent. The deposit is held in an account that earns interest, and will be returned to you when you move out, minus any repairs or costs to the landlord based on damage you caused.

Servicer (Student loans): An organization hired by a student loan lender to service your loan, including assisting borrowers, collecting payments, and maintaining records.

Stafford Loan (Student loans): A federal student loan, backed by the US government, that does not require payments while in college, with a 6-month grace period after you leave school or drop below half-time attendance before repayment begins. They are available as subsidized and unsubsidized.

State tax: Most states charge an income tax. This tax is deducted directly from your paycheck and usually represents between 5% and 10% of your income. You file a state tax return, similar to a federal tax return.

Student loan forgiveness programs: An optional benefit provided by certain companies, municipalities or other government employers designed to incent a college graduate to move to a certain locality or work in a certain sector of the economy. Tuition forgiveness programs are more common in health and education fields. They generally require a time commitment. The federal government also offers loan forgiveness on certain types of federal student loans for borrowers who enter certain types of occupations, such as teaching or public service.

Subsidized (Student loans): A federal student loan that is eligible to have interest paid by the federal government. Whether you are eligible for the interest subsidy is based on your financial need as determined by the federal government's Federal Application for Federal Student Aid (FAFSA).

Taxable income: The amount of net income used to calculate how much tax you owe.

Tenant: The person who rents a house or apartment from the owner.

Thrift Savings Plan (TSP): A retirement savings plan for civilian U.S. federal government employees and members of the uniformed services. The TSP is similar to the 401(k) plans for private sector employees.

Total income: Also called Gross Income, includes all of your income from your job, small business investments, interest or dividends received, etc.

Tuition reimbursement programs: An optional benefit provided by a company that reimburses employees for new courses they take, usually to contribute to their current position or company. The programs usually come with caveats such as remaining with the employer for a specific time period or maintaining a certain GPA.

Uninsurable: A person not capable of being insured or not eligible to be insured, usually due to pre-existing conditions, such as an identified chronic illness or disease.

Unsubsidized (Student loans): A student loan that is not eligible to have interest paid by the federal government. Whether you are eligible for an interest subsidy is based on your financial need as determined by the federal government's Federal Application for Federal Student Aid (FAFSA).

Upside-down: Also known as negative equity, refers to a situation where the value of an asset used to secure a loan is less than the outstanding loan balance. In other words you owe more on an item than the item is worth.

Value fund: A mutual fund that invests in companies that are determined to be currently priced below their otherwise perceived value based on specific financial measures.

W-2: The Form W-2, Wage and Tax statement for U.S. income taxes, is provided by employers to report wages paid to employees and payroll taxes withheld.

W-4: The Form W-4 for U.S. income taxes is used by employers to determine the correct amount of tax withholding to deduct from employees' wages.

Need More *Graduate's Guides*?

The Graduate's Guide to Life and Money is available
at quantity discounts for bulk purchases.
Visit *www.inceptia.org/books* for information.

Also available from Bill Pratt

*Extra Credit: The 7 Things Every College Student Needs to Know
About Credit, Debt & Ca$h*
This brief, easy-to-read book shows you:
- The top 10 ways credit card companies trick you.
- When to use debit cards and when to use cash.
- What is a credit score?
- How to choose the right student loan.
- And much more…

Newly updated with information on finding college financial aid and
choosing the best student loan. *Extra Credit* should be a mandatory book
for all college students.

Visit *www.inceptia.org/books* for ordering information.
Quantity discounts are available for bulk purchases.

Bill Pratt

Bill Pratt is the author of several books on personal finance including *The Graduate's Guide to Life and Money* and *How to Keep Your Kid from Moving Back Home after College* (June 2012), as well as a textbook on personal finance. His books help students and young adults improve their finances and their lives.

Bill is a former economist for the federal government and a former vice president for Citigroup. He left the financial industry to focus his efforts on helping others understand money.

Bill is Vice President of Viaticus, a financial education company. He is a college instructor at East Carolina University in Greenville, North Carolina, and Assistant Director of the ECU Financial Wellness Initiative. He also speaks professionally to college students and adults on topics ranging from money to careers. He holds an MBA in finance.

Bill's goal is to help students wade through the endless financial and life decisions they will encounter. By making the best decisions about life and money with the right attitude, Bill believes that people will accumulate more wealth faster and will then be able to use that wealth to improve the lives of those around them.

**Bill Pratt is also available to speak at your
school, company, organization, or association event.**

Bill Pratt
740 Greenville Blvd., Suite 400, #165
Greenville, NC 27858
301-788-2711
*info@ViaticusGroup.com * www.TheGraduatesGuide.com*

About Inceptia

Inceptia, a leading provider of financial success tools for young adults, is proud to collaborate with our colleague Bill Pratt, to bring you this useful guide to financial management. Inceptia believes strongly, that if applied, the principles in this book will help you lead an enriched financial life.

Together with esteemed author and financial expert Bill Pratt, Inceptia presents personal financial management seminars on campuses throughout the country. Inceptia's online financial education program teaches young adults the basics of financial management in an engaging environment. Inceptia is a passionate advocate for ensuring young adults of all backgrounds have access to the information, tools, and resources needed to understand their financial rights and responsibilities so that they can make informed financial decisions today and throughout their lives.

To learn more about how Inceptia can help you launch brilliant futures, call 888-529-2028 or visit *www.inceptia.org.*